Think Outside
the Box...
of Chocolates

*You never know when life
will be nutty*

By

Barb Miller

A-Argus Enterprises Inc
New Jersey***North Carolina

Think Outside the Box... of Chocolates © 2013 All rights reserved by Barb Miller

A-Argus Better Book Publishers, LLC
For information:
A-Argus Better Book Publishers, LLC
9001 Ridge Hill Street
Kernersville, North Carolina 27285
www.a-argusbooks.com

ISBN: 978-0-6158189-2-4
ISBN: 0-61588189-2-7

Book Cover designed by Barb Miller
Printed in the United States of America

Dedication & Acknowledgements

I dedicate this book to my mother and father for embracing the uniqueness of me, and to my siblings Ruth, Jeanne, and Dennis for loving me just the way I am. Also my husband Rod, for his support and love for all things quirky and creative that I have come up with throughout the years.

A special thanks to Rena Baker for her whip-cracking support and assistance with this project. A very big thanks to Val Harrison for her front cover photography of chocolates, and Peter Van Eunen for his fantastic artwork on the cover as well as the cartoons throughout the book.

About the Author

Barb Miller

Barb enjoys life with her husband Rod in the Okanagan region of British Columbia, Canada.

She has always been pathologically creative. As a child she started out with oil painting, then as she got older, that realm of creativity was not often used except for maybe a good game of Pictionary. In her thirties she joined a drama team where she acted and occasionally wrote short dramas. With her specialty being humor, there was a period in her life where she wrote and performed standup comedy. Now, her focus is mainly writing.

For her father's 85th birthday she wrote a children's book inspired by her childhood. She has also completed the second book in that series. What makes this interesting is that she never had children. She often says in jest, "I really don't write, as much as I take dictation from the voices in my head."

She is the youngest of four children and always knew that she was uniquely and wonderfully made. Growing up, this is how she was introduced by her parents: "These are our two daughters Ruth and Jeanne, this is our son Dennis, and this is Barbie". She had a classification all of her own. But what she came to discover is that she is not '*different*', she's quirky. By definition, the word '*quirky*' means: unconventional behavior. This definition may be in Webster's dictionary, but it is not biblical.

God created her exactly the way He intended, and by His standards, there's no such term as '*unconventional*'. Have you ever noticed that within the word '*creative*' is the word '*create*'? That's because our Creator, God, made each of us creative in our own distinct way. When we are ourselves, God loves it because we weren't programmed to be anybody else. This includes both someone that has a composed and logical personality to someone that has a more light and humorous perspective on life.

God happened to make her very creative. Since we are all made in His image, she is convinced that God is not only creative, but has a very good sense of humor too. She also believes that the writers of the Bible wrote by means of inspiration from God. She has experienced this herself in her own writing. She is often as equally amused with what ends up on paper as anyone else, because the ideas and words just seem to happen. Acknowledging and collaborating with inspired creativity gives way for her to honor God by using and sharing the talents He has given her. '*Think Outside the Box... of Chocolates*' is a collection of stories, poems, lyrics, devotionals and scripts inspired from when life is nutty to when it gives you chocolate covered nougats of wisdom.

<u>When Life is Nutty</u>

Don't ask me to teach Sunday School

I have never had a fondness for children, and vice versa. As a child I preferred stuffed animals over dolls. I was much more comfortable babysitting someone's dog than a child. Actually to this day, if you hand me a baby I break out into a sweat. With that said, back in the days of my youth there were very few means of serving the Lord in the church unless you sang in the choir, played a musical instrument, helped out in the nursery, or taught Sunday School. Well, I am not much of a singer, much to my mother's disappointment I don't play an instrument, and please don't ask me to help in the nursery or teach Sunday school. But wanting to be a good Christian I felt that of the choices available, being a church camp counselor would be the best bet for me. I thought that since the children were older and camp was only a week long, I could do my part for bringing in the kingdom and then go home. I ended up with preteen girls. When I recall that experience of being a camp counselor, the first thing that comes to mind is that when I get to heaven there will be some of those young campers I will need to apologize to.

The second thing is, that if I were to do it all again I would make it more spiritual for the girls.

Like every night before lights out we would have communion. And instead of the usual bread and grape juice, we would use Nyquil and Sominex. Come to think of it, starting the morning off with communion would also be a good idea.

Clapping Challenged

I was raised in a Baptist church back in the 60's and 70's. Church services have changed since that time. The style of worship singing now is more lively and casual. This includes garage band style music and clapping; lots of clapping. In my day there was a piano, an organ, and you held hymnals; making it virtually impossible to clap and sing at the same time. The first church I attended during this transitional style of worship was held in a gymnasium. Because the floor was cement, you could bring your coffee in with you during the service. This particular church even offered espresso coffee just like they have at the corner coffee stands. Most people during the singing would join in with both voice and clapping. In one regard it was wonderful because the music was so loud you couldn't hear one voice singing over another. So, I could totally enjoy this time of worship and would sing my heart out. Clapping and singing on the other hand is not something that I am capable of doing at the same time. You might say that I am '*clapping challenged'*.

It's a choice for me; either I concentrate on clapping or I sing. So to avoid the embarrassment of clapping off beat, I would cling to my coffee cup and sing away. You really shouldn't clap and sing at the same time while holding a cup of hot coffee. It's dangerous, don't do it.

But as the church grew, so did the need for a new building. In the new sanctuary there was a full stage and aisles and aisles of comfy chairs on a carpeted floor. Because of the carpet on the floor, bringing in your coffee during the service was banned. Now I faced the dilemma of singing or clapping. Being that I didn't think I could get away with faking a broken arm in a cast for very long, I ended up adapting. I even became more spiritual because instead of clapping while singing, I would just raise my hands in the air. Although I am not a great singer, I do love to sing. I am more of a car or shower singer. When I'm in my car and Steven Curtis Chapman comes on the radio, I crank it up, and like he sings in that song: "I'm diving in." This gave me an idea. I think there should be a designated section in the church sanctuary for car singers. To make it more comfortable for them, a steering wheel could be attached to the back of the chair in front of them. That way they can grip the steering wheel in front and sing away without being intimidated to clap at the same time. There could also be a section for the shower singers too. Maybe a good location for them would be under the sprinkler heads. But it should be made perfectly clear that clothing is still mandatory.

Turning Forty Was Ugly

It was coming up to my fortieth birthday and I was going to be ready for it. It was also time for my driver's license to be renewed. "Perfect, I will get my hair done and look beautiful for both my birthday and my driver's license pictures." Or so I thought. I went to see my regular hair stylist and asked for a haircut and a perm. Now just to let you know, I tend to have very sensitive skin and in the past have had some mild reactions to perm solutions. But the year before my hair dresser had used a brand of perm that not only curled my hair, it did not have any adverse reaction on my skin. So I made sure this time to ask that she use that same brand of perm from the year before. But instead she informed me that they no longer carried that brand and she would try something new. Being the trusting type and hoping for the best, I obliged. No sooner did the final rod come out of my hair; I could feel the burning sensation on my skin around my face. By the time I got home it had advanced to burning red lesions. I ended up going to an emergency walk-in clinic. After filling out the intake form and noting on it that I obviously had an allergy to perms, I am also allergic to Penicillin and Sulpha drugs. The doctor informed me that I indeed have second-degree burns and I was to go to the pharmacy to get a prescription filled for a cream to put on. He told me that by morning the inflammation should be doing much better. At the drug store I again made it known that I was allergic to Penicillin and Sulpha drugs. The Pharmacist handed me the prescribed cream and I went home to immediately apply it to my burning skin. The next morning my face was all puffy and red and my ears had swollen shut. Evidently the cream that he had given me had Sulpha drugs in it. This time I ended up in the hospital emergency room. They gave me a cortisone injection and sent me home with Tylenol 3's.

On the drive home from the hospital my husband informed me that for my fortieth birthday party he had invited about thirty people; some coming from as far away as

Seattle, Washington and Vancouver BC, Canada. Even though I looked like John Merrick from the movie The Elephant Man, I too was not an animal. Besides, I was on pain medication and cortisone, so as far as I was concerned the party could still go; just no pictures. The party took place as planned and even though a couple of my young nieces and nephews were scared to tears by looking at me, a good time was had by all. By the time I had my picture taken for my driver's license, my skin lesions had subsided and I was again completely recognizable. Fortunately for me, since that time straight hair has been in fashion. I must say that I look much better now than I did when I turned forty, because turning forty was ugly.

One time I tried to make a fashion statement that hairy legs could be beautiful. But I kept burning my leg with the curling iron.

Working for a Living

Veterinary Technician

(This job really bites)

In my life I have had many jobs. Naturally with my love for animals I went into Veterinary medicine and became a licensed Veterinary Technician. WARNING: This story may be offensive to some people. But if you are in the veterinary field or just have a sick sense of humor, go ahead and read on.

Part of working in a veterinary hospital involves euthanizing animals. It is just one of those aspects of the business. One day around lunch time all of the hospital staff were gone, except for me and the kennel girl. On my agenda that day was to euthanize a very old and very large dog. This dog must have weighed over 120 pounds. The procedure for such a task is to put the animal to sleep using lethal injection and then place it into a large plastic bag for the local humane society to come and pick up for disposal. These pick-up days were only scheduled for once a week so in the mean time, the dead animals in their plastic bags were placed in a freezer. In this particular hospital that freezer was down two flights of rickety stairs in the cellar. The two of us tried to manage carrying this dead weight but it was extremely awkward and heavy going down stairs. I was at the bottom holding onto the bag stepping backwards, and the kennel girl was at the top holding on to the bag trying her best to coordinate each step down with me. I don't quite know what happened, but somewhere half-way down these stairs the bottom of the bag broke and the lifeless body broke through and proceeded to thump down to the bottom of the stairs. Now don't think that I find that humorous at all (although you really sick people will be giggling right about now). No, the funny part to this story is that when that happened, the kennel girl stood up on the stairs holding the empty plastic bag and said "He's been having a hard time going down stairs."

Dog Groomer

(This job can get really hairy)

This is a story of a miracle. When I got home after a busy summer day of grooming dogs, I noticed that the large center stone of my wedding ring was missing. My heart sank and I immediately called the vet hospital where I was grooming to tell them not to throw the garbage out or use the tub at all, and that I would be right there. On the drive over I kept thinking to myself that the diamond probably rinsed down the drain of the tub and was gone forever. When I got there I checked the tub and the drain, but to no avail. With so many dogs being groomed on that day my routine was to just brush the hair onto the floor after each dog and only sweep it up after every two to three dogs groomed. This sweeping the hair from the table onto the floor action could have flung that diamond into any nook or cranny of the room. Although the highest possibility of the diamond's whereabouts would have been that it had washed down the drain into oblivion, I had to at least make the attempt to search for it in the garbage can full of dog hair. As I sifted through the dog hair bit by bit, and occasionally having to spray to kill the jumping fleas, I actually found the diamond! That, my dear friend, is a true miracle. So the moral of this story is: No matter how hairy life may get, miracles can still happen.

Phlebotomist

(this job really sucks, but I just like to needle people)

For those of you that don't know what a Phlebotomist is, it is someone that specializes in drawing blood. With my background as a veterinary technician, it was an easy transition for me to go from working with animals to working with people. Actually, vet techs make very good phlebotomists. Because having to find a vein through a coat of fur, one develops an ability to feel the vein rather than relying on sight alone. From years of working in a lab drawing blood, I began working as an insurance medical examiner. When people applied for life insurance, I would come out to their home and go over the questionnaire of medical history, do vital signs, draw their blood, and collect a urine sample. I loved it. I didn't have to work with doctors, sick people, or babies. There were a couple of very entertaining and memorable experiences from doing this job that to this day makes me smile. But then again, I am easily entertained.

Here are a few of those stories:

➢ Having a light and humorous approach to my job; I use a squishy rubber chicken for people to grip onto when I draw their blood. One time when I handed this chicken to a lady she said to me "very funny, did you do that just for me?" Had I paid attention to when I was writing down her name on the form, I would have noticed that her last name was Cluck. Yeah, now I think it's funny.

➢ One time there was a lady that was so nervous about having her blood drawn, I told her to start singing show tunes to take her mind off of it. No sooner did I insert the needle into her arm, she started singing "the blood will come out tomorrow…"

➢ Every insurance company has their own unique questionnaire form for the required medical history of the client. One day when I was asking the question relating to any history of drug use, one young man had a very amusing response. His response was that he smoked marijuana. But what made this funny was that the very next question was "For any reason do you believe you will take drugs in the future?" He then replied: "Yes, probably as soon as you leave." Then a few questions down it asked about alcohol use. He again said "yes" to this question and specified that he drank beer. The next question was "Have you ever reduced your consumption of alcohol?" He answered "Yes." Now the follow-up question to that was, "For what reason did you reduce your consumption of alcohol?" His answer made me laugh. He said "Because I switched to pot." Well, a few questions down asked "Have you had a weight gain or loss of ten pounds or more in the last year?" He said "Yes, I lost ten pounds." Now he must answer why there was a loss in weight. He explained "I switched from beer to pot and pot doesn't have as many calories as beer." *I love my job.*

Naturopathic Clinic

(where all the healthy people work)

For a while I worked as a receptionist at a Naturopathic clinic. There was also a Chiropractic practice and Massage Therapy business in the same building. Considering that I was overweight and thought that running late is a form of exercise, I felt a little out of place in this job where all the healthy people worked. I felt shamed into drinking my Mountain Dew out of a brown paper bag. One day I made the mistake of telling one of my co-workers that I was hungry. She politely offered me one of her rice cakes. Now I don't know about you, but I can think of better uses for rice cakes than eating them. I don't think she noticed when I used it for a coaster for my tall Mocha with Macadamia nut with a splash of caramel latte. They could be used as absorbent shoe inserts, or you could even cut them down and use them as pads for corns on your feet. With just a little pressure they can also take those nasty scuff marks off your kitchen floor. Over time I think I finally got the people there convinced that chocolate is one of the food groups. Being that chocolate comes from the cocoa bean, and beans are a legume, it's really a protein. That goes for coffee and jelly beans too. So next time you order a mocha anything from your favorite coffee stand, give yourself a star for making such a healthy beverage choice.

Working in this kind of environment tends to bring in people of a certain lifestyle and philosophy. I would often get posed the question from patients "so, what is your sign?" Being that I believe that God is in control of our life's plan, horoscopes and the like are not something I take much interest in. But for these people your astrological sign had a lot to do with who you were. So in order to appease them, I would just say that I was born under the sign of the shopping cart with the wonky wheel. Because let's face it, when you look up at the stars at night they all basically look like assorted styles and sizes of shopping carts. There is the Fisher Price one, the flat bed trolley

kind, and of course the shopping cart with
the wonky wheel.

Sewing is Not My Gift

With the name Barbie, you'd think that growing up I would have had a Barbie doll. My two sisters Ruth and Jeanne had Barbie dolls. My two sisters also have the gift of sewing. Their Barbie dolls were of course, fashion models and they would sew them beautiful and elaborate outfits. I had a Midge doll, and I don't have the gift of sewing. The extent of my sewing ability for making doll clothes was to cut the toe end off a sock and shove it over her body. I was making tube dresses long before they were in fashion. With this kind of wardrobe, my Midge doll was not equipped to be a model, so I made her a nun. I called her Mother McCree. Thinking back to that now, maybe the outfits I made her weren't quite appropriate for a nun; being that they were all short and strapless.

But my mother still thought that I should take sewing lessons. She enrolled me in the local Singer Sewing School. Did I mention that sewing is not my gift? Once I got past the step that you had to reach behind the needle and flip down the lever so that once you started sewing the thread wouldn't wad up, I could manage a pretty descent seam. But my best sewing skill was that of seam ripping. I totally understand why they called that device in the back of the machine the tension knob.

Still hoping that I had a domestic thread for sewing, my mother got me a sewing machine for a Christmas present the first year I was married. Having not yet come to terms that sewing just was not my gift; the next year I decided to sew a pair of pajamas for my husband for Christmas. Not just any cotton or flannel pajamas either, no, I wanted to make him silky ones from a fabric called Kiana. Personally, I think that the name Kiana must come from an ancient language which translates into the word "Satanic." This material had a way of being swallowed by the sewing machine which consequently required the damaged material to be cut off. After getting through the repairs of reconfiguring the pant legs so that they both faced down, I was almost near completion of this project of love.

Then the time came for the final touch of sewing on the lapel pocket. Why they have these pockets on pajamas, I will never know. I don't know if it was because this task was on a smaller scale than the rest of the pajamas, but attaching the pocket turned out to be much harder that I thought it would be. With each failed attempt I would have to rip and repair the fabric until that poor pocket ended up being more like the size of a pen holder for one pen. Again, why would you even need to carry a pen in pajamas? So, I sewed on a decal of his initials instead. He said he loved them. He never wore them, but he loved the love that it took to make them.

Spiritual Gifts Not Mentioned
in the Bible

The Bible tells us that we as Christians are all given spiritual gifts. I have identified in my life a couple of gifts that are not mentioned in the Bible. They happen so often that I do believe it is supernatural. Although not in the Bible, my guess is that they must be documented on some Dead Sea scroll scriptures not yet discovered. One of these gifts is the ability to heal cars. For instance, I can be driving down the freeway and see off in the distance a car that has pulled over and is parked on the shoulder. Who knows how long they have been stranded there and have not been able to get their car running. As soon as I get close to them, they miraculously are able to start their car up again, pull out in front of me, and drive on ahead very slow. So if you are ever in the position where your car won't start, don't bother calling the auto club for assistance, just call me. Watch for me in your rear view mirror. As soon as you see me coming, go ahead and start the engine, then pull out in front of me. This phenomenon also seems to happen to me with busses. I have not yet figured out the purpose of this gift but feel that in some way God has used me for good whenever it happens.

I have never been a good speller. I am very creative and tend to take that creativity into my spelling as well. I can even give Spell Check a run for its money as to what word I am trying to spell. It just isn't right that in a world that doesn't even spell phonetically *fonetically*, there should be such hard and fast rules about everyone spelling the same way. Then one day I had the insight that it's not that I can't spell, it's that I have the gift of spelling in tongues. It just takes someone with the gift of interpretation to decipher the words that I spell. So those of you that are spelling police, don't be so quick to point out my misspellings, don't be judgmental, or be so quick to correct me. Work with me and realize that you must have the parallel gift of interpretation. Consider it sanctioned by God for being able to reveal the correct spelling.

There is also another phenomenon that happens to me all of the time. It is not what I would consider a gift of sorts though. As a matter of fact, this one confuses me. What happens is that when I am in the produce section of the grocery store, invariably the misters will turn on and I end up getting wet. Now I believe in immersion baptism, and that the act of public expressing one's decision to be a Christ follower is not intended to be more than a one-time deal. So I don't quite understand God's purpose in this sprinkling every time I go to the grocery store. I just know that every time it happens, afterwards I feel like having communion and going to a potluck dinner.

My Husband Plays the Accordion

One time I did a warm-up comedy routine at a Frank Marocco Accordion event in Mesa Arizona. Regardless of the fact that it was for an accordion workshop, I thought that Arizona would be a lovely place to be in January. The crowd for this event was accordion players and their spouses. When gathered at the tables together for meals, conversation was pretty much dominated by accordion players. If you don't play the accordion or speak their lingo, this can make mealtime quite boring. There would be name dropping of famous accordion players; none of which would ever be the answer to any People's magazine crossword puzzle.

I devised and shared a technique to help me, and those like me, to get through the evening. When someone started talking accordion, which of course made no sense to me at all; at the end of their sentence I would, in my head, tag on the line: "if you know what I mean." It can be very entertaining. Plus, the results are a slight grin on my face which in turn makes me look like I am involved and enjoying the conversation. For instance take the sentence "I told Elka that she had to fix the leak in my bellows before the evening performance"... if you know what I mean. The spouses in the audience not only appreciated this technique, but at the next meal as I looked around the room I could tell that they were putting it to use. Along with this bit of advice, I shared with them this piece you are about to read, which I had written earlier that day.

The Loves of Our Lives

"I love the rainy nights, I love the rainy nights, I love the rainy nights." Okay, Eddie—we get it. That phrase seems to multiply as the song goes on. Maybe it's just the nature of the writer... Eddie Rabbit.

I grew up in Seattle and I must say that I DON'T like the rainy nights, or the rainy day after day after day. I don't like walking in the rain or singing in the rain. But for some reason I do like the sound of rain when it comes from my 'sleep sound' machine. Go figure.

"I love _____" It's a phrase we hear all of the time. Things like "I love the snow" or "I love the sun." People will say about me that I love dogs. But let it be known that I also love chocolate, cheesecake, and a good cup of coffee. The way I see it, chocolate and coffee are made from beans, and beans are a legume. Cheesecake is made with cheese and eggs which accounts for both a protein and a dairy. If you put fruit on top it fulfills yet another daily food group serving. At least all of my vices are healthy.

Perhaps the word *'love'* isn't quite right for such things. For instance, some people love bagpipes, while others may say that they love the accordion. Often the term love is really a person's passion. My husband loves me and has a passion for the accordion. So much so, that on our twenty fifth wedding anniversary he was in Kimberly, British Columbia for the annual accordion festival. Because I love him, I relish in the fun he has when he plays the accordion. That's the difference between love and passion. Passion is a personal thing that you do for yourself. Love encompasses having a passion for someone else's joy.

Being married to an accordion player, writing comedy comes easy for me; especially after I've had more than a few Gin and Diatonics. But seriously, accordion playing is both a skill and an art, and for some it is even a gift. After thirty three years of listening to all kinds of accordion music, I have come to appreciate the happy music only an accordion can deliver. But, what I appreciate more is when I see the therapeutic joy my husband experiences when playing the accordion or when he gets together with his fellow bellows brothers. During Oktoberfest season I have become an accordion widow. For my husband, playing the accordion is his passion. But, I am the one he loves and we intend to share our passions together for the rest of our lives.

Hot Date

I bet at one time or another you have thought to yourself "Where would an accordion playing husband take his wife on a hot date?" Well, I'll tell you. First of all, Rod loves pasta, and the Olive Garden restaurant had just opened in our town offering all you can eat pasta and salad. I happen to love olives, so when I heard the name Olive Garden I got excited thinking of all those olives.

When I was a child and there were olives offered at a holiday dinner, I would put an olive on each of my fingers and pop them individually into my mouth. But when we got to the *'never ending;* Olive Garden salad, there were only two olives in the whole thing, and you had to fish through the salad to find them. To me that is just a blatant misrepresentation of the name Olive Garden. If they are going to be doing that they should just call their restaurant The Olive.

After dinner we went to see a musical group called the Canadian Brass. It is an ensemble of a trumpet, trombone, and a tuba. Don't get me wrong, if you are a musician this is an awesome group to go see. But I'm not a musician and Rod had tried to tell me that they were hilarious and I would love them. I thought he meant funny ha ha. Anyway, we went to the Mount Baker theatre where we were the youngest in the crowd standing in line for this. I'm sure that we were also the only ones not being a card carrying recipient of social security benefits.

For a crowd of this age they did have some interesting things at the concession stand though. There were the Ensure lattes… those were good. Then they had chocolate covered Coumadin. I really wanted to try those but you had to have a doctor's prescription to get them. There were these adorable Pez dispensers in the shape of paramedics that would dispense Nitro glycerine tablets from their mouths. But again, you had to have a prescription to buy them.

You know how at some concerts they will turn the bright lights out into the audience? Well, with this crowd it maybe wasn't such a good idea; they all got up and started heading towards the light.

Which reminds me; I don't think I'm quite ready to have a DNR (do not resuscitate) code on my medical records. But I do want to have the code DADW (do all dental work) on my chart. So if I am admitted into the hospital in a coma; bring in a dentist and have him do all the dental work he can possibly do. That way if I make it, it will have made the coma worth the while. If I don't make it I will have a nice smile.

I own a pair of high heel stiletto shoes, but the only time I wear them is when the lawn needs aerating.

Better Late Than Never

While at the pool one day, I was talking to a woman who was also there because of a New Year's resolution. Except this year, she decided to take the guilt out of any possible failure and keep it positive. Her New Year's resolution was "better late than never." It was the first day of March and she had just gotten out her cards for the now past Christmas holiday... *better late than never.*

It got me to thinking just how this new approach to resolutions would work.

I will start telling members of my family that I love them every time I see them... *better late than never.*

This year I will eat right, drink more water, and exercise... *better late than never.*

I will floss my teeth at least once a day... *better late than never.*

I will de-clutter my house by taking on one room at a time... *better late than never.*

I will take pictures of those items I always thought should be sold and list them on eBay... *better late than never*.

When the oil light comes on in my car, I will take it in for service sometime that same week... *better late than never*.

But now the fuel light did come on in my car... *better late than never?*

I will get gas in the car tomorrow... *better late than never. Oh* no.

When I get the renewal notice for AAA, I will send the check in as soon as possible... *better late than never?* Darn.

I will charge my cell phone when I see the battery is low... *better late than.* Oh crud.

Now by the time I walk two miles in the pouring rain to the nearest gas station and back to my car to put the gas in so I can get to the AAA office to renew my road side assistance policy before it closes; I still have to drive to the Jiffy Lube place for an oil change before it closes too. Hopefully I will still be able to make it to the store to pick up fresh fruit, vegetables, bottled water, and rice cakes. But by then the Dairy Queen will be closed. Better hold off getting the oil change for tomorrow… that can't be a good sound from my engine. So much for *better late than never*.

"But your sign says you close at nine o'clock; it's one minute to, and I have just walked all the way from the Jiffy Lube place where my car died and I need a Chocolate Caramel Fudge Lava Sundae please."

It is never better to be too late for Dairy Queen. Especially after a day of resolutions gone horribly bad. Tomorrow I will eat right and drink water… *it's better late than never.*

Weight Just a Minute

Every year my New Year's resolution is to lose weight. So in a way it is not so much a resolution but rather more like an annual tradition. And true to form (pun intended) I fail. But I have found that it is all in the wording. If I say "I *want* to lose weight" I can do that, and actually be very successful at it.

I have had a weight problem all of my life. At least I'm past the age where I would get asked the question, "so, when are you due?" My response has been "Well, I'm not sure. I have been gestating this for years now. If I could induce labor and push it out I would." I even had one of those unique Hollywood names for it; I would call it Lipo.

Where I live now it can get blistering hot in the summer. Now you'd think that in that kind of heat I would sweat like a pig. No, my body prefers to retain water. It is amazing how on a hot day I can wake up a perfect size 9 and by the end of the day I am well into the double digits.

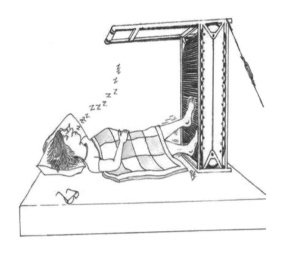

Is restless leg syndrome considered a form of exercise?

Bugs Bug Me

I think bees are good creatures. They are on a specific mission and pretty much mind their own business. But, I don't think there should be another dime spent on any space expeditions to the Moon, Mars, or any other planet until they solve some of the problems here on earth. Problems like yellow jackets. I know homeland security is important; but maybe we could direct some of those funds into protecting us from these miniature flying terrorists. Just as in the twin towers, these malicious insects can and will attack when least expected. Think of all of the vehicular tragedies that have been caused by the car being invaded by a yellow jacket that caused the driver to abandon safety for self protection. No, I think that those moon launch monies should be spent on saving human lives from these killers here on earth.

On the other hand, it could very well be a spiritual battle and yellow jackets are Satan's tools to inflict fear, terror, and pain in attempts to get us to swear. I'm surprised that they were not mentioned in any of Frank Peretti's books.

Bee Murder Cold Case Reopened

While on my walk today I suddenly noticed that a bee was following me, and at times even circling me. I wondered why I was the target of this deliberate behavior. Then it dawned on me that this could very well be a special agent from the Bee Police on a hot lead stemming from years ago. The case in question involved me and a bee back in 1963 when I was six years old. After being stung by a bee I took a Mason jar in hand and proceeded to go out to the garden with the sole purpose of incarcerating as many bees as I could and seal them in the jar. My thoughts were that I would eliminate all future threats of being stung again by a bee, or at least minimize the chances.

But as it is 49 years later, I have had no further criminal intent on annihilating the bee population. In my life I have come to realize that bees have a very definite and honorable purpose. Besides, I have lived in Canada for over five years now and the bee murder incident happened in the United States. With that in mind, I didn't understand how this bee could think that there was any possibility of extraditing me, or the fact that at the time of the incident I was a minor. I thought that after all these years; surely the statute of limitations must have expired by now. It wasn't long until that bee must have realized these same facts and gave up on the chase. But if by chance there is ever a bee in the car with me while I'm driving; it's either him or me and I will not hesitate to kill again.

Child Labor

(I Must Be Doing Something Wrong)

I don't understand the deal with child labor. We had my husband's teenage niece and her friend stay with us one summer for two weeks. Not ever having any children, I thought the idea of child labor would be of great help for getting some things done around the house. I guess I'm not doing it right because it wasn't working.

First of all, I have noticed that it is a lot more expensive to buy groceries for teenagers than it is buying food for my dogs. Mind you, the selection for my dogs is only one kind of food and I only feed them twice a day. I am not one of them, but some people who also have never had children like to put clothes on their dogs. Even then, the amount of clothing for a dog is limited to one, maybe two sweaters. If the dog were to somehow get the sweater off, it is still only one piece of clothing lying around the house to pick up, and definitely not any shoes, socks, or other unmentionables.

True, I do have to pick up after my dogs in other ways on a daily basis. But, there is the differing advantage that I can legally lock them up in one room in order to limit the amount of damage they may do while I am gone.

You would think that teenage children would be far more advanced in understanding and responding to verbal commands than dogs. I think one of the key differences here is the term 'command' verses 'request'. Either way, for the most part when I ask my dogs to 'come' or to 'wait', they know what that means and will do as they are told. A dog's whole focus in life is to please you; whereas a teenager will generally only focus on what you have to say to them when it has to do with pleasing them in some way. This is where I must be doing something wrong with this notion of using child labor. As I recall, growing up when my mother asked us to clean the house, we did it. Plus, we were not only expected to complete our task at hand in a reasonable amount of time; the end result was to be sufficient if not excellent. We did not get paid for these chores either, in turn we were fed, clothed, housed, and were allowed to watch TV.

If only there was a game app to program into a teenager's phone that made it so that their only means of advancement is if they were to actually complete a task in the real world. And, the imbedded 'parental control' must first give approval upon completion of the given chore in order for their phone to continue to function. This might make a good modern day study similar to that of the research involving Pavlov's dogs. You see, dogs and children are very similar. Although the whole electric shock for negative behavior would probably be frowned on. I guess it's a good thing that I never had any children; but I make a good aunt.

Christian School

From kindergarten through high school I attended Seattle Christian School. It was an environment that was very conservative to say the least. The librarian there would even screen the incoming magazines for any scantily clothed women. She would then color dresses on them with a black felt pen before she put them out for viewing.

Then there were the spot checks for skirt length, making sure that there was only two inches from the floor to the bottom of the skirt. For this, all of the girls were called out of class to be lined up on their knees in the library for their skirt length to be measured. If only Velcro had been invented back then, it would have been so simple to start out dressed modestly and then with one quick rip, become very stylish. I don't know who invented Velcro, but my suspicions are that it was a rebellious teenage girl that went to a Christian school.

You'd think that from a school like this a major percentage of students would go on to Bible school or even become missionaries. But oddly enough, many went into the fashion industry. Go figure.

Where Everybody Knows Your Name

I have to admit, I am terrible at remembering people's names. I've tried that method of associating their name with something familiar that will bring to mind their name the next time I see them. But, then I forget that reference that was supposed to help me remember the name in the first place.

I work in the medical field where confidentiality is a hard and fast rule of the profession. I figure that this memory loss is more like a built in confidentiality. They can try to torture it out of me, but I will never reveal your name to anyone.

I think that not being able to remember someone's name is genetic. As I recall growing up, my mother would at times call me by one of my sister's names, and on occasion even call me by my brother's name. Now that we are all grown, I have seen it in my sister when she has addressed me with her daughter's name and vice versa. With this in mind, I do believe that this is some kind of inherent disorder that I really have no control of. So if you really want to go somewhere where everyone knows your name... wear a name tag. By the way, look up the lyrics to the theme song from the TV sitcom Cheers; they are hilarious.

Pursuit of the Perfect Purse

It seems in life that men are forever chasing golf balls, a plaid shirt that is almost identical to the others they already have, or the next new car smell. Women, on the other hand, are in constant pursuit of the perfect purse.

I sit here in a chair looking at a collection of used purses laid out on a table at our garage sale. I recall how each served a purpose at one time in my life. They provided not only a practical means of portable storage with an impressive amount of pockets and compartments, but also was an attempt to make some sort of personal fashion statement. If asked, I could not specify why any one of those purses inevitably was emptied and put high on the shelf in the closet. I can't explain why I continue to tolerate my current purse that has only one pocket, but otherwise is just a bottomless pit. They should make an "app" for locating items in your purse. But that would only work if I could actually find my phone that is lost somewhere in the black hole that is my purse. Come to think of it, I do know why I still put up with that particular purse. Yes, it is stylish and when I first saw it, somehow it spoke to me that it was the perfect purse for me. The only plausible reason I could think of would be that of pure destiny. But, the real reason that I continue to use this purse is because it brings back the memories that come with it when I bought it.

A couple of years ago we were in New York City with my sister and her family. We were daring the New York adventure of shopping for underground black market designer purses. Having navigated Canal Street before, my sister knew just the right winks and nods it took to connect with the sales people that would guide us past the store fronts and down into the secret chambers of wholesale brand name purses. The game was to play the shopper that is unwilling to accept the ticket price and even go so far as to make the move of walking away. This of course, prompted the last ditch effort of bargaining for a price that would not only seal the deal, but make for the best stories of the trip. My sister, and her soon to be daughter-in-law, bought a couple of purses for a fraction of the cost of retail. They nonchalantly surfaced back onto the street carrying their contraband in the telltale black plastic bags that indicated to all of the other black market dealers that they were "players."

That experience in itself was a blast, but I really didn't need a purse and up to that point had no reason to buy one. While we continued our journey through the purse stores of Canal Street, we walked into a small unobtrusive store displaying more purses that pretty much looked like all of the other purses that we had seen so far; except for that "one" purse. For some reason I was drawn to it. Nobody else in the group paid any attention to it. I picked it up and threw it over my shoulder; it just felt right. I put it back on the shelf and tried to convince myself that even at that ridiculously low price, I didn't need a purse. I started to walk away, but somehow felt compelled to turn around and look at it just one more time. I figured that since I did not turn into a pillar of salt, it was God's will that I buy that purse after all.

As of today, I still use this purse. Oh, some day another purse will come along and out of necessity due to wear and tear I will need to buy another purse. But until such time, I will continue to dive for keys, pens, floss, and the like that are buried deep in the bottom of this purse. You see, every time I pick up that purse it takes me back in my mind to Canal Street and all of the precious times shared there with my sister and family. Some day in the future there will come another garage sale where I will lay this purse onto the table and attach to it a piece of masking tape with a price on it. Maybe when that day comes someone else will see that purse and for whatever reason it will speak to them.

You know that old saying: "garage sales are one man's junk but another man's treasure"?

I don't think of it as 'junk', but rather just closure to treasured memories that are about to take on a new story when someone else takes home their own newly found 'treasure'.

The Phone Books of Our Lives

Whether it is a Dex, McPherson, or whatever local phone book you may have in your area; like clockwork every year a new and updated phone book will be sitting at your front door. There is an old ad slogan that goes "let your fingers do the walking." This suggests that you can find anything you are looking for by merely two stepping with your fingers across the yellow pages of the phone book.

For the same sort of convenient reference, most homes also have a more personal self made phone book. These are readily available to purchase at any pharmacy or business supply store and come in a variety of sizes and colors. They all have alphabetically tabbed section dividers and the pages are lined for neat and organized use. But if you are like me, our home phone book *(since ours is the color gold, we refer to it as the gold book)* is anything but neat and organized.

Unlike the mass distributed commercial phone book, our home phone book does not get updated every year. It will instead get added to from time to time. But, with this added information also comes scratched out numbers, scribbled in new numbers, and names and numbers written on Post It notes stuck to pages. Also in our phone book, those alphabetical tabs may or may not give lead to information necessarily beginning with that particular letter of the alphabet.

Quite often numbers would be stored under the letter of someone's first name simply because I can't remember their last name, or never knew it to begin with. A phone number may be listed under the letter "C" for cousins. This is where you will find the names and numbers of my cousins. Those blank dividing pages that hold the alphabetical letter tag, also make very good scratch paper for while you are talking to someone on the phone. For instance, I know I can always go back to the "C" page and find the cookie recipe that my Dad gave me years ago. Plus, along with an assortment of Chinese food and pizza menus of restaurants from all of the towns that we have lived in, the front and back inside pockets are bulging with pages of typed phone lists from fire departments and churches dating back to 1980.

Yes, our phone book has seen its day. But, it is a collection of friends and family of our lives that can also be considered a time capsule of sorts. Leafing through the menus and listings of people and businesses that are assembled in this tattered and dated phone book, I can recall the times and places of our life lived. This sort of organized chaos is indicative of why I don't scrapbook or why I rarely have my Christmas shopping done until December 24th.

Oh, I could go out and get a new home phone book and transfer names and numbers from the old one to achieve an updated and current source of information. But, I like to think of it as growing older together. Just as there is more room in the cover pockets and pages of that old phone book, there is still room in our lives for more new friends and family that will come with changing names, phone numbers, and restaurants with takeout menus.

A Place Where Time Stands Still

I would never have thought that there is such a place where time stands still, but I think I have been there. Come to think of it, I have been there in the past as well. Now I even question myself as to whether I am still there and all that has happened to me in life has just been a dream and I never actually left that place at all. Because today I found myself in that same place again where it felt like time stood still. Of course I am talking about the checkout line at Michael's craft store.

I don't know what it is about the checkout clerks at Michael's, but every time I have to endure that long line of waiting, they always seem to take foreverrrrr.

And to stay true to form, today was no different. After waiting for I don't know how long, I was finally the next in line. But that is when the forces of nature took over and time stopped dead as the person in front of me dumps out about twelve items and two receipts with the request for a refund. The clerk proceeded to punch something into the cash register and begins to scan the items. What followed did not happen in real time but rather seemed to be more in slow motion. The customer and the agent exchanged possible means of refunding the items by separating

But this was not the products with the correlating receipts. to be the end of this return transaction. Next, the clerk dropped her chin and began to speak into the small microphone attached to her shirt and makes a request for anyone in the store to help her. When there was no response, she repeated the request with an additional plea for help because she had never actually made a return before. The manager finally showed up. But his assistance was brief and minimal because I guess it was part of her initial training to work under pressure and figure these things out on her own. The customer was actually of more help than the manager and finally between the two of them the refund transaction was successful.

Finally I was next. Before I knew it, the cosmic force of time took over and I found myself paying for my items with one dollar bills, nickels, and pennies. Again the phenomenon of time stopping was in play but this time the target was that of the next person in line behind me.

The moral of this story is: If you plan on doing any shopping at Michael's craft store, go ahead and prepare dinner for the evening using the crock pot. It will be done by the time you get home.

New Year's Resolution

As time demands, my calendar is going to change to another year in January and New Year's resolutions are the question of the day. As of today, there is nothing that can be done for all that I did or did not do in the previous year. But, the prospect of another year to set new standards in my life totally leaves me torn. I'm all for self-improvement, but history has shown that I am not one for discipline. The annual resolution is to lose weight. So far my only consistent discipline is to avoid weighing myself at all cost. Before you know it, another year has gone and that speculated goal of determination compromises into being repeated on the next year's resolution list.

No, this year I am NOT going to make any New Year's resolutions. I am going to make New Months' resolutions. I'm really not good at math at all, but if I make a resolution every month, after twelve months I will have made a year of resolutions without all that demand of daunting consistency. This way if I succeed or fail, I will always have the next month to set a new goal or even the same goal.

So for this new January, I will strive to lose weight by going to the gym two to three times a week; even if only just to use the hot tub. I will try to make healthier choices of what I eat, and drink more water. I will write more, with the goal of writing that second children's book that everyone is waiting for before their children reach adulthood. Actually, I could write while in the hot tub and for that matter, I figure that just sitting in water has to have some hydrating qualities to it that should count for my daily water intake.

As far as for eating stuff that is healthy; I figure that if you heat something to a hot enough level it kills germs. So just imagine how much better something is for you if you fry it in hot oil.

It's good to take it slow at first. There's always next month.

I Have This to Say About That

Where Stop Signs are Just a Suggestion

I recently moved to a new town in a new country. Yes, they all still drive on the right hand side of the road, and the steering wheels are where they should be. But, the driving patterns are very different here from where I came from. I'm not a city girl, and the town I came from was small. We always had a freeway and before I left, we even had a Costco and some of those roundabouts at intersections. By comparison, this new town would be about the same size; maybe even a bit smaller. It also has a Costco, and even though it doesn't have a freeway with overpasses, it does have a highway running through the town. In the beginning the driving here surprised me and many times even scared me. Cars would simply consider stop signs as just a suggestion. As far as I could tell, there was this 'as long as I'm first' attitude that was the driving force for this self-absorbed driving behavior. Along with not stopping at stop signs, at least two or three cars would run red lights through intersections.

I had to adapt to a survival of the fittest mentality just in order to turn left. Part of my frustration was that if an intersection had one of the few actual left hand turn signals, it would only be green for about eight seconds. Allowing for the cars to clear the intersection that have run their red light, you only ended up with two maybe three cars able to turn with the left turn green signal before it was back to waiting for a fleeting moment to cross left through the oncoming traffic. I don't like that kind of pressure or degree of risk when I drive.

I also observed manoeuvres that I had never seen before I moved here. One of those moves involves utilizing the two way center turn lane as a passing lane. Also, if you have the audacity to stop and signal to make a left turn onto a side street, the cars behind you will then use the shoulder as a passing lane. What really almost caused me to consider prescription drugs, was if I was driving down a road and there were no cars behind me and I could see ahead of me a car waiting on a side street to enter into my lane. One would think that with no cars behind me, they would wait the three seconds it would take for me to pass by them so they could freely enter behind me. But it seemed to me that they would sit there and wait until I got closer, then pull out in front of me only to then drive slow. Finally I came to grips with this dilemma when I was reminded of the scripture in the Bible that says "the first shall be last and the last shall be first." Now I consider myself blessed on a daily basis when I drive in this town.

You would think that with this entire disregard for the rules of the road the local police would be cracking down on red lights runners, vehicles that drive through stop signs, cars that merge over three lanes all in one unchecked movement, or cars that use the shoulder as passing lanes. Sadly; not so much. As far as I can tell, there are only two rules that merit any kind of consistent enforcement in this town. Those are: wear your seat belt, and drive dead slow in school zones. The police here fervently set up radar screenings in school zones and surveillance sights for checking to see if you are wearing your seat belt or not. So, when I see a car running a light or making a left turn from a right hand lane, but they are wearing their seat belt; from what I have observed, there is no need for alarm - everything is just fine.

As if all of that mayhem on the road isn't frustrating enough, the behavior of motorists in the parking lots has me on the verge of acting out that scene from Fried Green Tomatoes and just ramming the idiots. It again takes that attitude of "I'm first" by drivers taking no heed to cars backing out of parking stalls. One can be backing out and be three quarters of the way out when another car, at risk of being hit, will simply dart around the backing car so that they won't actually have to stop. Even though I now expect this behavior, I still will shake my head in disbelief for such a lack of intelligence or courtesy. But, I put the blame on video games. When you think of it, video games condition one's thought process to avoid any objects that might pull out in front of you, and to dodge around past them or you won't ever make it to the next level. I think to reverse this behavior; video games should make it so that when something comes out at you, you actually get points for courtesy by stopping for it. If you insist on risking it and drive around anyway, you blow up.

In this video game of life, I choose to be the good guy. So if you are merging onto the freeway I will let you in, or if you really need to be first, I will let you go in front of me. But if you insist on driving behind me when I'm backing out of a parking space,

one of these days I might just snap and ram
you anyway.

If I were a bird I think I would choose to fly over moving cars instead of swooping down in front of them.

Raising Dogs verses Children

I never had children. I raised dogs. I may joke that with raising dogs you can legally lock them up, they will never borrow the car, they really have no desire to have a cell phone, and without opposing thumbs, you will never hear them practicing an instrument.

I have had some dogs that attended obedience school. But the only supplies I needed for them were a collar, leash, and cut up pieces of cheese. I never had to fight the school supply crowds at Wal-Mart for back packs and assorted school supplies, because I would just use the same collar and leash over and over again through the years for each dog that went to a class. For each dog, Fall fashion was always pretty much covered by its own natural hair coat. Although there were years where I did need to go shopping for Halloween costumes and festive attire Santa Paws pictures.

Oh, I am fully aware that with both dogs and children one must care for and pick up after them on a daily basis. But, with dogs I only have to feed them twice a day and they use the same dish. Now that I am in my fifties I realize what I am missing. While at the store I find myself drawn to a child and just have to go up to them and ask if they would be so kind as to program my cell phone for me. My dogs are of no help with any modern day technology. I have even been tempted to ask a child's mother if they would allow their child to come over to my house for a day because I have some files and pictures on my computer that I need saved to a flash drive I don't have because my dogs don't have any idea of how to do that.

I Hate Rounded Corners

I have been guilty of watching a lot of those home makeover type shows on HGTV. When we decided to sell our house I was particularly interested in the shows that included projects that we could incorporate in our own remodel. Well, after about two years and thousands of dollars later, I have seen the light. That light is the blinding manipulative brainwashing of those shows that are sponsored by home hardware stores and the like.

Not only do they give the prospects of completing such transitions in two to seven days, they also have access to much more funds and skilled labor than we do. These shows repetitively give the impression that if your house does not have granite counter tops and stainless steel appliances it is a piece of junk.

This granite counter top thing has all of the mass hysteria that the pet rock had in the seventies. It's a slab of polished rock that will cost you anywhere from six to ten thousand dollars for your kitchen counter alone. Personally, my kitchen is not that impressive in the first place. I think that it matters more what comes out of your kitchen that should make a good impression, not the work surface of your culinary creations.

We have been going with the ever popular neutral theme to all of our colors and accessories in order to give that appropriate appeal to prospective buyers. Are we part of a dying breed that when looking for a house to buy, we actually see the potential and possibilities beyond the color scheme or need for new flooring? Again, I blame those shows for creating the demand for "move in ready." Don't get me started with the power of the anal retentive house inspectors either. I think if they went into a spanking brand new building that had passed all of its inspections; they would still come up with a six page list of questionable needs for repair.

One thing I have learned is that I will never again own a home with walls that have rounded corners. They are very attractive until you decide to paint the adjoining room another color. Now you have to create a straight line all down the bend in the doorway that leads to the next room. Then there is the hair pulling task of putting painters tape on that rounded edge from top to bottom in order to paint the one room's color up to it. Then pull the tape off so you can see that beautiful line you created. At this point you are feeling pretty pleased with yourself. So, you then repeat the taping and painting process on the other side with another color. Wait a good twenty four hours to dry because you don't want to pull the tape off too soon.

The next day with full anticipation, you pull the painter's tape off with visions of a perfect straight line dividing the two rooms of complimentary colors. Even though you pull the tape ever so slowly and gently, to your dismay the paint underneath pulls from the first wall that you painted. After you re-tape and patch paint those spots you confidently pull the tape off only to realize that the tape has again pulled the paint off the wall. I think you get the gist of my nightmare.

My guess is that the Architect that designed rounded corners must be in the witness protection program somewhere because if I knew where he lived I'd kill him.

With all that we have done in preparation to make that winning impression to buyers, I can't help but think that if this house should go up for sale again in twenty years from now, there will be people coming through and either saying out loud or to themselves "this place is so 2010." And so the insanity continues.

I don't have a green thumb. The only flowers I have in my house are either plastic or dead. I have more like a gangrene thumb.

Fitness Isn't Fair

You know how you feel right after you've eaten too much, or within a twenty four hour period you realize that you have successfully polished off an entire pan of Rice Krispie treats? You not only feel bloated, you look bloated too, and your pants immediately become tight. What's not fair is that after spending one or more hours of strenuous sweat-worthy exercise, your body does not immediately reflect your efforts. Your clothes don't fit any better until this exercise has been consistently repeated for weeks. I wish I could come up with a better moral to this story, but fitness just isn't fair.

God Made Night People Too

I am not a morning person. I can stay up till one or two o'clock in the morning no problem. Now before you morning people get all righteous on me, let me point out that the Bible backs me up with the reality that there are night people too.

Proverbs 27:14 *(Good News Version)*

"You might as well curse your friend as to wake them up early in the morning with a loud noise."

I'm going to get a little prophetic here and suggest that the "loud noise" means that of the phone ringing before ten o'clock in the morning. So, morning people, get off your high horse because if it weren't for night people like me, there would be no such thing as brunch.

Differences Between Men and Women

It's a fact, men and women are genetically different. Men have "Y" chromosomes and women have "X" chromosomes. It is these "Y" chromosomes that make men more muscular and, by stereotypical standards, more mechanically inclined. What boggles my mind is that even though they have the strength to loosen bolts in an engine and take it apart as well as put it back together again, they can't seem to have the strength or mechanical ability to accomplish the technical maneuver of that simple spring action it takes to change the toilet paper roll.

It is a fact that because of this "Y" chromosome, men have a higher chance of being color blind than women. I think this could very well be a factor in another vision related deficiency that men in general have exhibited. For instance, have you ever noticed your husband can be standing in front of an open kitchen cupboard and call out "where's the peanut butter?" (or you fill in the blank here), even though the peanut butter is right there in front of him? Ladies, when that happens, I urge you not to get upset, and don't try to talk him through it from the other room. It's that "Y" (pronounced "why") chromosome that genetically makes it impossible for him to find things that are right in front of him. That's why there have been all kinds of inventions to aid men in this area; like the label maker and design plans to outline the different tools on the wall of the garage. Save your frustration and just go in there and get for him the item he can't seem to see. It is important though that you leave the room before you laugh or shake your head in disbelief. Just remember that he genetically can't help it.

I have also observed that men tend to have more gas than women. This can pose a real dilemma when it comes to sleeping in the same bed. So here is my solution: When at night there comes wafting from under the covers a malodorous gas; reach over to your night stand for a jar of Vick's Vapor rub and slightly dab some around each of each of your nostrils. Trust me, you will thank me later. This has been such a lifesaver for restful sleep; I give Vick's Vapor rub as a bridal shower gift. I will wrap up a large jar as well as a convenient travel size too.

Oh Canada

Although I was born and raised in Seattle my heritage is not only Canadian, I married one. When I was young we would often go to see our grandparents who lived in Vancouver, British Columbia. I remember some of the differences of the two countries that would stir excitement in me with anticipation of our next trip to Canada. Those things were that grape pop was called '*raisin*', the rich and creamy delight of a Jersey Milk chocolate bar, and my favorite being an Eatmore bar. Since these were only available in Canada, it was a real treat every time we went up there. Now that I live in Canada, I can eat Eatmores whenever I want. That unfortunately tends to add more to me than I would like, if you know what I mean. If only I could like a candy bar that looks good, smells good, but tasted awful. They could call it an Eatless bar.

Living here, I still can't get over the inflated price of cheese. I have now become like one of those Canadians that smuggles cheese and dairy products across the border on a regular basis. I found a good deception was to tuck a block of cheese inside each shoulder of my coat. If the border crossing agent had any suspicions, I would just explain to him that I didn't have any cheese; these are shoulder pads.

Fruit Basket Upset

In the summer when I was a child I would earn money by picking strawberries. Well, mostly I was eating the strawberries I picked because they were just so soft, sweet, juicy, and around for only a short time. But I still managed to make enough money to go down to the drug store to buy a pack of Double Bubble or a Popsicle from the ice cream truck. I would ride my bike within a five mile radius of home, and after taking a short hike through the woods; my sister and I would lay in the sun on the sandy beach of the local river.

As small children, on weekends we would hang our heads out the back window of the family station wagon as we went for a Sunday drive. These scenic drives would often include a visit to the Tastee Freeze for some soft ice cream which would invariably drip melted ice cream all over us from the bottom of the disintegrating cones. In order to keep us entertained on longer trips, we were challenged by our mother to watch for deer and/or bears. If that distraction did not work and the noise level in the car increased, we were warned that if we did not quiet down, the wheels of the car would fall off.

Childhood experiences now are nothing like those that we as children were able to enjoy in the fifties and sixties. Now it is unheard of for a child to ride their bike beyond yelling distance of their home, or ever to be seen on a bike without a government approved safety helmet. For a child to walk through the woods or swim in the river and sunbathe on its banks without parental supervision is just asking for an amber alert. Leisurely Sunday drives with the children are rarely done now beyond the years of needing to take them for a ride in the car in order for them to fall asleep. Even then, between the seat-belt buckling and the car seat installation, it's more like preparing for a space craft moon launch than a short trip to the grocery store. As the age of these passengers increases, for their amusement there are now in many vehicles the option of offering an "in flight" movie. Unlike air travel, electronic devices are allowed in vehicles, which results in multiple sound effects from dinging and bleeping to zapping death explosions. In the case of any devices used for listening to music, and I use that term *music* lightly, at least ear pieces are available and highly recommended. While Dairy Queen is still a great stop for frozen delights, kids today no longer have the choice of having a butterscotch dipped ice cream cone. Or maybe I should say an artificially flavored butterscotch hydrogenated palm oil dipped non-dairy frozen substance cone. The one thing that hasn't changed in that regard is that ice cream still ends up dripping through the bottom of the disintegrating cone.

Apparently all of these changes have come for the good and safety of our children. But there are some things that have changed from those days that should, by nature, have remained the same. I'm talking about the fact that strawberries are supposed to be soft, sweet, and juicy, not crunchy and tasteless. Peaches are supposed to be soft and flavorful, not crunchy. Apples on the other hand, are supposed to be crunchy, sweet, and juicy, not soft and mushy. My only assumption is that these adaptations to the texture and tastes of fruits are a result of manipulating nature for the purpose of making speed to market for higher profit margins. Children can learn and experience history by going to a museum where they can see what things used to be like. Wouldn't it be nice if they could go to a museum and experience what fruit used to smell, feel, and taste like?

"P" is for Perfect

1)   Pizza crust - I am always looking for the perfect pizza crust recipe.

2)   Profession - It is always a good thing to find that perfect profession that you can shine in.

3)   Pillow - So far all of the pillows I ever had just don't measure up.

4)   Phone - They make phones now that are smarter than me.

5)   Pen - Whether it be from your desk or in your purse, if given a choice of pens you will always show preference of one over the others.

6)   Porridge - Even the three bears were pursuing the perfect hot cereal.

7)   Purse - The perfect purse does not necessarily involve pursuit, but rather it finds you.

8) Present - What do you get that person that has everything? Or, what do you get a teenager? Oh wait, there is a perfect present for that… cash.

9) Pill - Whether it is for an aching joint or an aching head, one is always looking for that perfect pill to relieve what ails you.

10) Paint - You have decided on a color to paint a room in your house. You go down to the hardware store to get paint. But now you are faced with a wall full of little cards that have slightly varying shades of color. After about thirty minutes, you have narrowed it down to the card color choice that just keeps jumping out at you. But then after painting that color on the wall, it really isn't the right tone you were hoping for. So you either live with it, or you go down to the store again and select yet another paint color to paint over what you thought was the perfect color in the first place.

But when it comes right down to it, the ultimate 'P' in your pursuit for the perfect whatever, really stands for 'personal'. That, my friend, has everything to do with Y.O.U. and you will know it when you find it.

Party On

A few weeks ago we had some friends over to the house. In our conversation, somehow the topic of birthdays came up. We were all sharing when our birthdays were when one gal said that her birthday was April 26th. With that said, her husband mumbled a correction that her real birthday was in late November. To that she explained that her actual birthday was in November but she was never fond of having a birthday party in the cold and miserable weather that November usually has. She later in life decided that she would much rather have her birthday celebration take place outside when it is warm, comfortable and more suitable for a party that includes barbecuing. Besides, late in the fall people's time and attention is more geared towards making ready for the Christmas holiday season.

I say "Good for you!" and "Why not?" There is evidence of a historical nature that indicates Jesus was not actually born in December. Yet, we have made his birthday on December 25th. As a youth I recall celebrating President's day in honor of three different US presidents as a separate day off for each one of them. Somehow over time the decision was made to combine all three president's birthdays into one Monday in February. If the powers that be can mandate birthdays to days of the calendar in order to suite the need for a three day weekend, why is it that Thanksgiving is still always on a Thursday?

The moral of this story is: Regardless of what month and/or day you were actually born, the day that you celebrate it is just a decision away. I say "Party On!"

Last night I had to come inside when the mosquitoes got too bad. In the morning I woke up with bites all over my legs. It all makes sense to me now, because when I was on the deck I could have sworn I heard a tiny little voice saying:

"Moe Skitto and family, table for three?"

Slow Computer Games

Our computer is so slow.

How slow is it?

It is so slow, I do believe we have Windows Jurassic version.

Here are some fun computer games you can play while using your extremely slow computer:

1) Go make a cup of tea and see if it gets done before your screen changes.

2) Run a hot bath. Make sure that the water is hotter than desired so that by the time you have finished working on your computer, it will have cooled off to just the right temperature. I suggest that you also have a glass of wine while you are waiting. This is for if the bath water ends up cooling down too much; you will still feel relaxed and warm.

3) Practice changing a tire.

4) Read the book War and Peace.

5) Take a laxative and see which one moves first.

Not Your Ordinary Devotionals

Separation Anxiety

I had a dog one time that was a bit on the insecure side. Because of this he became obsessed with a need to be with me at all times. As much as I tried to impress on him that I was only going to be gone for a short while and that I would soon be back, being a dog, he didn't understand a word I said. He only new that one minute I was there and the next I was gone. They call it separation anxiety. When left alone, or even when with another dog, he would become anxious to the point of frenzy. With his mind in a panic over my absence, he would dig at the door or find anything of size to pull away and chew into pieces. He would usually choose to destroy either a magazine or a paper product of some kind. Even when confined to a kennel, he would gnaw on the chain link and often push against the bar of the door bending it enough to squeeze out. Then he would sit at the door waiting for me to come back.

From what I understand, toddlers at a certain age will also go through a separation anxiety when they lose sight of their mother. Although I have never had children, I have witnessed the screaming terror of a child realizing that his mother is no longer in the room. For the most part children will grow out of this and eventually get to an age when they actually prefer that their mother not be around them at all. Dogs emotionally remain at the age of a human toddler. They make drugs now to help reduce the stress of separation anxiety in dogs, but it comes at the cost of semi-sedation.

Sometimes I feel like I have separation anxiety when it comes to God. I know He loves me and I have experienced a true relationship with Him in many deep and spiritual ways. His physical absence in my life at times becomes a frustration. I also know that He has promised that He will come back and we will be forever together. But, I still sit and look out my life's front window and can't help but feel the anxiety of anticipation for the physical reality of His presence. I've always heard things like "God is in control", and "It is all in God's timing." God knows that in the big picture of things it won't be long, and there will come a time when there will never be any separation. When my dog frets over my not being there, I don't find out till I see him again to realize how he chose to handle his stress. But God in His power and position can see me in my times of stress and knows of my separation anxiety. I'm sure He really doesn't want me to chew things up, sit and stare at the door, or from an earthly perspective, at the cosmic eternity of the sky. He knew that this sort of thing might happen. That is why He implanted in us the Holy Spirit. It's that internal nudging that tells me to stop staring at the door and enjoy life for what it is. I've got a good home, a loving family, and the ability to have fun and enjoy life.

I'm also reminded of the separation anxiety I had as a child when I went to summer camp. I didn't want to go, but my Mom and Dad told me that I would have fun and that they would pick me up at the end of the week. Soon after meeting new friends, rowing boats across the lake, and roasting marshmallows under the stars, that anxiety of leaving home never entered my mind. Well, this world is like one big camp. There are new friends around every corner, lots of arts and crafts, and there is always the promise of home at the end. Whenever I get that feeling of separation anxiety, the Holy Spirit sits me down and tells me that I should go and have fun, my Father will be there to pick me up at the end of camp.

Do You Think God Would Like Bowling?

God in His nature is relational. We as Christians strive to practice numerous disciplines in our lives in order to attain spiritual growth. Have you ever thought of the verse in Psalms that says "Delight in the Lord, and he will give you the desires of your heart"? I got to thinking of that word 'delight'. Webster's dictionary defines it as "something giving great pleasure." The word itself requires the corners of your mouth to turn up. I think that God desires to be included in the fun things in our lives too.

The very fact that Christ's first miracle was performed at a party indicates that maybe, if they had them back then, he could have been on a bowling league. Just for the fun of it.

Personally, I show dogs for fun. I know there are only a select few that will be able to relate to my story, but hang in there with me; I think you will catch my drift. I was scheduled to go to a show and my dog that I was intending to show decided to go on a hunger strike two weeks before the show. I had tried the Choo Choo game with the spoon, and even made special chicken pot pie to entice him to eat for mommy, but nothing was working. Being a male dog, he had other priorities at the time, and eating wasn't one of them. The show day came and I fluffed his hair coat as much as I could in order to try to conceal his lean body flesh. Even though I got him to look good, his lack of appetite caused yet another hindrance to showing. In the show ring in order to stimulate expression and attention in the dog, the handler uses food as bait. With a dog that had no desire for food, needless to say, his attitude was essentially flat. But this for me is my quintessential golf game and my sport of fun. So, I invited God to join me in the show ring, and we will do just that…. have fun.

Five minutes before going into the ring I tried one last time to entice my dog with some bait hoping he would show some spark. After having refused food for two weeks, to my surprise, he scarfed it down like it was the best stuff he had ever eaten, and wanted more! We went into the ring and he showed like a trooper. We placed fourth out of fourteen. I gave him a big hug, accepted our ribbon and as soon as we left the ring I offered him a treat for doing so well. He flatly turned it down! As a matter of fact, for the next two days he again refused to eat. But what I did realize is that for those ten minutes that I was in the ring showing my dog, God gave him an appetite! Not that giving a dog an appetite is as impressive of a miracle as turning water into wine, but God added his contribution to our showing together. Just as the wine miracle allowed the party to go on, since God was personally invited to enjoy the dog show with me, He just did what he could to help the show go on. My biggest thrill for that day wasn't getting fourth place in a dog show, it was that God partnered with me and the realization of that made the fun of showing my dog awesome. It can be a real delight when you share your fun with God. I think He thoroughly enjoys the intimacy of sharing it with you too.

Maybe your hobby for fun is golfing, sailing, quilting, woodworking, or searching for treasures at garage sales. Whatever it is, take delight in the Lord and share the joy of it with Him. If He can change water to wine, just imagine what pleasure it would give Him when you putt that perfect hole, or find just the right fabric for that special quilt, or even make that spare that tips your bowling score into the three digit range for the first time.

Yes, I think if He could be on your team and be a part of your fun, God would really like bowling.

It's Good to Be Easily Hoped

In regards to a certain circumstance, someone said to me the other day "Don't get your hopes up". That got me to thinking. What an awful thing to say to someone. I am easily hoped and think that having hope is a very good and healthy state of mind to live in. Actually if you don't have hope, you are pretty much hooped on having a positive attitude in life. So don't let anyone rob you from that window of time of hoping that something wonderful might just happen. The worse thing that could happen is that it won't happen and that only means it wasn't meant to happen. Simply turn the page and engage in the next thing that will get your hopes up, because it is just a funner way to live life.

Clean Us Up When We Are Dirty

You know how sometimes when you are reading a good book, something in that book hits your soul with such illuminating impact, it is like the feeling you get when you step out of the tub from a long relaxing bath. You breathe in with your eyes closed, and with the slightest upward tilt to one side of your mouth, you open your eyes and breathe out with a sigh of contentment. Your body and soul taps into a self-awareness that you needed, and it feels good. Well, unlike the inner good feeling from a relaxing bath, the revelations learned from the pages of a book can be passed on. Now a days they not only can be passed on by sharing them with a loved one or a close friend, they can be beamed across the world to limitless friends and strangers alike via the internet. It kind of gives a whole new meaning to Facebook. Even though I cannot see you face to face, I can share "ah ha" moments that I experience as they happen while the "ah" effect is still at its peak, and before the "ha" effect has even set in.

Well, this morning while reading from the pages of Philip Yancey's book A Skeptic's Guide To Faith, I chose to put my book marker in between the pages to save my place, and closed the book so I could breath in with my eyes closed, and with my eyes open breathe out with a little sigh of enlightenment.

He wrote about how the reality of sin is not to lead us to the Judgement Throne, and having succumbed to weakness or rebellion and sinned; God is actually pleased that we come with confessions of failure. Not because He was just waiting for you to mess up and now you have some major sucking up to do to gain His love and attention. No, the mere fact that we feel guilty at all from our ill-behavior has been planted into our makeup so that we not only become aware of sin, but we are compelled to come to God for damage control.

Such accumulation of sin has no other direction to go than away from relations with God. Just ask Adam and Eve. God's intention is that we don't "let it ride" with un-confessed sin, which will in the long run lead to consequences of self destruction. Instead of a relational clause requiring perfection, God awaits your repentance with love as an opportunity for healing and renewal.

In Phillip Yancy's book he shares of a mother's son that was asked by his baby sitter as to what his Mommy's favorite thing to do with him was. The little boy responded by saying his Mommy's favorite thing was to "clean me up". When his mother was told of his answer to this question she responded "In truth, that isn't my favorite thing to do with my son. Cleaning him up is an excuse for me to hold him." So it is with our heavenly Father. After all, He went through a lot of pain, suffering, and death on a cross so that those sins would be covered. Because of His relationship with us through Christ, He sees us only as His treasured children. As far as "cleaning us up when we are dirty," it is His opportunity to hold us.

Need a Jump?

Years ago I attended a one-day voice over workshop in downtown Vancouver, British Columbia. With the intent to drive somewhere for lunch, I went out to my car that I had parallel parked on a one way street.

Evidently I had failed to turn off my headlights when I parked there that morning and now my car wouldn't start because the battery was dead. I walked a few blocks down to a gas station on the corner. As I was heading toward the gas station office to ask for some help, a big black macho type 4x4 truck pulled into the gas pump area. I thought for sure that with a rig like that, surely they would have some jumper cables.

Out of the truck steps a stereotypical 'biker chick' complete with leather jacket and tattoos. I approached her and asked for her help. She replied that she would get to me in just a minute. She then proceeded to go over to a guy in a car parked at one of the other pump stations. She grabbed him by the collar and aggressively pulled him out and shoved him against the hood of his car. She was screaming and cursing at him and after releasing him with a swift shove, she started to walk towards me. Within those few steps she collected herself and told me that she was ready to give my car a jump and asked where my car was parked.

After giving her directions to my car, I left the gas station and went to raise the hood and stand by my stranded vehicle. Soon a car pulled up and parked behind my car; followed by the big black truck. With jumper cables in hand, the biker chick again pulled this guy out of his car, shoved the cables into his hands and pushed him towards my car. I asked if I could help in any way. Her response was "No honey, I wouldn't want you to electrocute yourself, and I don't want to get electrocuted, if anyone is to be electrocuted it will be this #@&%."

As he is hooking up the jumper cables to the battery of my car, she is cursing and yelling at him about how she now understood why the bills kept going unpaid... that money was going up his nose with drugs. She paused and leans over to tell me "okay honey, start her up." My car started right up. After the dust had settled with the feuding couple, I was compelled to give this young woman some means of appreciation for her help amidst the present turmoil that she was facing in her life. All I had on me was a Canadian twenty dollar bill. So I took her hand and gave her the money with my gratitude for her kindness. She grabbed me and gave me a hug. Through tears she said "You have no idea how much this means to me right now."

Well, after what I had just witnessed I not only could tell that she needed the money, but I also sensed that God had purposely put me and my dead battery there at that time to bless this young woman. I got in my car and paused to thank the Lord that number one, I didn't get killed, and number two, that He had made Himself evident to me in that situation.

I had gotten up that morning with an agenda of going to a workshop for voice over. But as it turned out, I ended up in a workshop for hearing God's voice without really even knowing it until it was all over and obvious. The Bible describes Christians as being vessels. This little story goes to show that you never know when you will be the vessel for God's purpose. Sometimes you won't even realize it until you notice that the flowers He puts into the vessel come to life right before your eyes.

Once In A Lifetime

A few years ago, those members of the Oprah show's studio audience that received a new car can certainly rank that as a "once in a blue moon" kind of experience. In other words, it was definitely a "once in a lifetime" happening. Let's face it; remarkable and real events in our life's journey affect us much more than the sight of a fictitious blue moon ever could.

"Once in a lifetime"… for some reason that phrase has its own unwritten rule. That rule is that the experience that happens is always an extraordinarily good one. If we think long and hard enough, we can all bring up a memory of an occasion that resulted in such surprise or awe, we feel that the chances of it happening to us again would be slim to none. But such a positive result could also be associated with personally escaping tragedy or even death. Under extreme and dangerous conditions for some miraculous reason you survived. It is in those cases that one would just as soon keep that kind of experience to once in a lifetime.

The word "miraculous" often is mentioned when speaking of phenomenal circumstances. When repeating those stories from our lives, we still shake our heads in unbelievable gratitude of what happened to us. Of course it happened, but it didn't just happen without reason or purpose.

The fact is, unbelievable things happen to all of us at one time or another. We may even be responsible for being a part of someone else's "once in a lifetime" experience and not even know it. It could be that day a twenty dollar bill fell out of your back pocket and was discovered on the street by a struggling single mother. That miraculous provision then becomes her once in a lifetime story. On the other hand, it could be that one day you slept through your alarm and missed your plane. That plane that you were supposed to be on flew into the Twin Towers. Sure, you may at some time in your life sleep through another alarm, or even again miss a plane. But, that fateful day for so many will remain your miracle.

The bottom line is that we all live our lives only once. For each of us wonderful things will happen and awful things will happen. But don't for a minute think that any of it happens without our Creator not only being there, but also has full knowledge of every detail that is your life. The Bible tells of a very specific "once in a lifetime" experience that Jesus had that offers us today a once in a lifetime decision to make. It's no surprise, and it will definitely never happen again. It's a once in a lifetime guarantee that will forever change the rest of your life.

Po-M&M's and Laughable Lyrics

Ode to the Donut

*(Lyrics of a song from the movie
The Sound of Pastry)*

*Dough, a smear, a glazed top tier
Cake, a hole in center fun.
Me, I can't control myself
I choose the lemon centered one.
Goo, in middle of the bread.
Nuts, on top the frosting head.
With these, the pounds I will not shed.
Which will bring us back to dough, oh,
oh, oh.*

Stuff I Think About

(Stuff I think about and wonder if any-one else thinks the same)

Like if God has another name for me,
what would it be?
I just know that He loves me too much
to let it end in "ie."
And if there's a mansion in heaven,
what in heaven's name will I do?
I guess the party's at my place.
Yes, that would be heaven for me with
you.
I hope to walk and talk with Him.
But can it ever be, with all the sum of
saints to come
For His time to be with only me?
He hears us now in unison, and knows
what we can't see.
And when it's no longer prayer but talk,
will we actually be side by side and
walk?
These questions I ponder of these things
up there and yonder.

I think God must be grinning in His lov-
ing care,
And patiently waiting 'cause He knows
I'll know once I'm there.

He May Not Be Handy, but
He's Handsome

(I wrote this one for my husband. Let it be said that he is handy as well as handsome. He just is not cut out (pun intended) for woodworking. But he can take apart an accordion and put it back together again... let's just see any carpenter try to do that.)

Other lady's men may build them
a chair or a couch
Or a roof on top their house.
Maybe my man not so much,
But he's got his own magic touch.
He's got that cute factor going on
That makes me melt down to my toes.
God only knows, he may not be handy
But he's handsome.
His idea of woodwork is measure twice
cut once,
And go get more lumber.
Oh he's got the tools
He's got the pouch
All it takes to nail it

But as far as he's concerned
If you can buy it; makes no sense to
make it.
He's got that cute factor going on
That makes me melt down to my toes
God only knows
He may be not be handy but he's hand-
some.
Don't get me wrong, he's a good man.
He makes me coffee in the morning;
like the good books says he should -
right there in Hebrews.
Oh, maybe not with wood
But he's good, he's good.
He's got that cute factor going on
That melts me down to my toes.
God only knows
He may not be handy but he's handsome

Blah, Blah, Blah, Blog

Blah, blah, blah blog
Blog about the weather
Blog about the fog
Blog about the kids with their Labra-
doodle dog.
Talking on paper like a diary in a way
Writing of family life for family far
away.
It means a lot to you
And to them it means much more.
But for us who follow blogs
It reads nothing but a bore.
It can be all for fun
But not fun for all.
A choice must be made to read some at
all.
Give me blogs with humor
With insights into life;
How doing things the wrong way can
turn out being right.
Or cooking with real butter
Makes lighter into like.

Stories for the sake of stories
Is not my cup of tea.
Unless of course I really am your pre-
cious Aunt Bea.
So blog on about this
Or blah blog on about that.
Just saying it's only some that keep me
coming back.

If a rolling stone gathers no moss, why is it that a whirling ceiling fan gathers so much dust?

Paws the Night Before Christmas

Twas the night before Christmas
and all through the house
Were squeak toys and dog hair
'cause it's a dog's house.
The stockings were hung by the chim-
ney to see
The holes in the toes were suspicious of
those
But their sad eyes cried "wasn't me."
The dogs were nestled all snug in our
bed
While visions of Santa Paws danced in
their heads.
The jolly old dog that no-one can see
Knows just what they want
Includes popcorn tossed while watching
TV.
On Dasher, on Dancer
On Comet and Vixen
On Cupid, on Donder
and watch out for Blitzen.
But the most flavorful reindeer of all
Is the one on the treat box for dogs

marked venison that is kept in the hall.
Yes, twas the night before Christmas
And in the morning they'd see
That jolly old dog
Has always been me.
There for their good times, and there for
their bad.
It's them here for me that makes my life
glad.
So cuddle them
Hug them
And throw them a bone.
With them here for Christmas we'll
never be alone.
Merry Christmas, and to all a woof-
night.

Rod's Poem

(First, here is a little background for you so you will understand this poem:

1)   I am not a morning person

2)   I don't know why, but while walking, I prefer to walk on Rod's left side. Maybe it is because I'm a dog lover and there is something about being in the heel position that I just feel more balanced.

3)   When it comes to tuna fish sandwiches, I like mine made with just mayonnaise; nothing else.

4)   We never had kids, we raised dogs.

5) My favorite movie of all time is Babe - the movie about a talking pig that thinks he is a sheepdog.

Roses are red
And chocolates will do.
But what I find sweet are the things
you don't do.

You don't turn on the lights when
you get up at dawn,
And you walk on my right
'cause you know my left is just all
wrong.
You don't pepper the tuna till my
sandwich is spread,
And you don't mind at all
When the dogs jump on the bed.
The remote you don't grip
When through the channels you flip,
You just hand it to me and say "here
hon. You pick."
You'll watch with me my favorite
movie
And won't hold back the tears,
Because after all, that pig did de-
serve all those cheers.
Oh, don't get me wrong,
I love the things you do do.
But it's the things you don't do
"That'll do, pig, that'll do."

Thyme in a Bottle

(To the tune of the song Time in a Bottle by Jim Croce)

If I could put thyme in a bottle
The first thing that I'd like to do
Is embellish you with all of your joys
and dreams
'cause you give always for all, not for
you.
I know that we'll live in forever
We'll clap in thyme and dance the day
through.
Our prayers and our tears have been
saved through the years
By the one through His blood we'll be
made new.
If I had a box full of pictures
Of the fun times we've shared me and
you,
The box would be full to the brim and I
know
The memories you would scrap book
them too.
But there never seems to be enough
thyme

To do the things I want to do
With my sister
I've looked around enough to know
That you're a friend I want to go
through thyme with.
(I put these lyrics on a label that I put
on the side of a clear bottle with
a sprig of Thyme sealed in it, and gave
it to my sister for her birthday.)

The Apostle Paul's Journey

(To the tune of the theme song from the TV show Guiligan's Island)

Just sit right back and you'll hear a tale
A tale of Paul's three trips
That started from Selucia, a port of An-
tioch
A port of Antioch.
Paul's shipmate was his buddy
Barnabus
And Mark came with them too.
These passengers set sail that day
For a two year journey
A two year journey… that turned into
eight.
The weather started getting rough
The tiny ship was tossed
If they had only listened to Paul's ad-
vice
The trip wouldn't have been so long
The trip wouldn't have been so long.

The ship took ground on the shore of
this land of pagans and Jews
With Elymas… the sorcerer
Barnabas, and sometimes Luke
The Galatians, Thessalonians, and
Church of Corinth
All in Paul's three journeys.

So this is the tale of our Apostle Paul
He was gone for a long long time.
He had to make the best of things
Not bad for doing time, not bad for do-
ing time.

He taught their best wasn't good enough
Christ died to save all lives
But it made the Jews uncomfortable
They chose to close their eyes
They chose to close their eyes.

No commandments, no idols, no special
law
Not a single hierarchy.
Like Moses to the rest of us
Christ came to save all lives
Christ came to save all lives.

So join us here in the book of Acts
You're sure to get a smile
From three guys just obeying God
From seas to lands of isles.

HRT Theme Song

(Hormone Relief Telethon)

(To the tune of theme song written by Michael Jackson in 1985 for the charity telethon benefiting the African famine at that time)

.

We are the women

We have the hormones.

We can make a better day,

Or make you miserable.

Misplaced my keys,

Can't find my car now.

But give a little time

And I'll turn on the charm now.

We are the women

We have the hormones

We can make a better day

Or make you miserable.

My moods can swing

From high to low now.

There are more words to this song

But I can't remember them.

When I was young I always wanted to have a year-round tan. Now that I am in my fifties, I do but it is in patches.

<u>Sit Right Back and I'll Tell a Tale</u>

I Don't Know if I Can Take
Another Week of This

Oh look, it's raining. It has been raining every day this week. I know that's why we can enjoy the beautiful green lush lawns and thriving gardens. But, that green comes at the cost of wet dog smell, muddy footprints, wet clothes, and a daily schedule of mad dashes from the car to the nearest indoors. For Pete's sake, it's summer! If it doesn't stop raining I feel that a case of the blues will be coming on real soon. I don't know if I can stand another week of this. Plus, I have totally run out of ideas for macaroni art projects for the two little ones to do. Then to top it all off, they want macaroni and cheese for breakfast, lunch, and dinner. Well, with a week's worth of pasta art projects piling up, I am not going to just throw those sculptures away. No, I plan on scraping the macaroni off the paper into boiling water which will melt the glue right off. Then any paint that washes off is absorbed into the macaroni.

The only problem is, whenever one of my kids goes for a sleepover, they'll ask their friend's mom if she ever makes "rainbow" macaroni like their mom does. When invariably I am asked by these mothers the question of where I get "rainbow" macaroni, I just tell them that I have a second cousin that works in the Kraft test kitchen in Pennsylvania. I then will explain to them that since the "rainbow" concept did not meet the necessary approval ratings, my cousin let me have some of the limited stock that will never reach the grocery store shelf. Just for good measure I throw in that I promised that I would only use it for my own family.

Oh look, it's not raining today. The skies are blue, the birds are singing and once again children on bikes are riding past on their way to friend's houses to go inside and play video games. There will always be tomorrow to vacuum and do laundry. It's so beautiful outside I think I will make myself a cup of tea and turn to chapter two of that book I borrowed from my sister four months ago.

It's another gorgeous day out there. The forecast for this week is sunshine and hot temperatures. Time to get out the tank top and garden gloves, there is a good hour of weed pulling to do out there. But first, I must make a gallon of ice tea and pour fruit juice into Tupperware freeziepop molds. Ah, I love summer.

"Kids, put the sprinklers on in the garden and in an hour switch it to the front lawn. After that, you can wash the car. It's so dusty you can write on it. By the way, who wrote 'I'm too dirty for my car' on the back window? When it cools down, that lawn needs to be mowed. And don't forget to put sunscreen on before you go outside. I'm going down to Wal-Mart to get another fan; I'll be back in about an hour."

It is too hot today to do anything. I just want to sit here in front of the fan with my ice tea and read a book. Laundry and vacuuming will have to wait until it cools off. Or, I'll do it when the kids get home from swimming when there will be no clean towels or dry clothes left in the house. It's too hot to cook. I guess we'll have pizza again tonight. I'm thinking if we just let the lawn die we won't have to water it every day or mow it every four days. I don't know if I can stand another week of this heat.

Oh look, it's raining today… yeah!

All the World is a Stage

"Come on in, Nell, and thanks for picking those up for me." Gloria said as she stepped aside to let in her best friend. "How many did you get? I'm so nervous. I've been up since three. Do you want some coffee? I've already drank a whole pot, but I can make another one if you want. Oh forget the coffee. I'll make it after I read them. No, I can't. Please, could you read them to me?"

Nell gently took Gloria by the hand and led her to the couch and as requested began to read the first review. "This one is from Variety: '*I saw no prodigy in last nights Broadway play Prodigy of Baker Street. Along with this play's lack of depth or continuity, lead actor Jason Arlen and supporting actress Gloria Holden's performances were as unremarkable as the play itself*'. Forget this one." Nell said as she nonchalantly placed the paper on the floor behind her. "Don't let that bother you Glo, I heard that a lot of these critics don't even go to the plays they write about anyway. They just thrive on being nasty."

Nell pulled up from the stack the next paper. "Here, The New York Daily News has a much better reputation; let's see what they have to say. '*Prodigy of Baker Street opened last night with expectations of another hit from writer, director Matthew Holloway. But unfortunately the plot line and drab script of this play left me only to realize that, unlike Holloway's last play Hit and a Miss, this was one is definitely amiss.*' Yada, yada, yada, okay, here...'*Gloria Holden who played supporting actress to lead actor Jason Arlen, tried her best to deliver her lines, but between the two of them this three act play dragged on rendering it mildly entertaining at best.*' "Now see, he saw that you tried. It's not your fault the writing sucked."

"How many more are there?" Gloria questioned Nell as she closed her eyes, tipped her head back, and squinted with reserved anticipation.

"There are just two more. Hang in there Gloria. I was there and thought you did great. This one is from the Chicago Times *'Broadway saw the opening of a new play by Matthew Holloway last night called Prodigy of Baker Street. Quite frankly, this play should be running in some little theatre/bowling alley on Baker Street in Small Town USA, not on Broadway in New York City. The weak and flimsy story line was matched only by mediocre acting'."* Nell quickly tried to salvage any dignity left from that last statement by saying "I'm sure that he didn't mention your name because he thought that even the best of actors couldn't have saved this play." But Gloria still couldn't help but hang her head and sigh.

"Gloria, this is the last one. Do you want me to read it?" Nell asked. "Go ahead. If it isn't any better than the others, I have an emergency bag of M&M's in the cupboard if we need them." Gloria said as she held back her tears.

Nell began to read from the last paper. "This review is on the front cover! *'The play Prodigy of Baker Street opened last night on*

Broadway. From the moment the curtain opened, my breath was taken away by the outstanding performance of this play's supporting actress Gloria Holden. I could not take my eyes off of her as she delivered every line with dramatic passion and sincerity'. Gloria, this guy really loves you! Wait, there's more. '*This beautiful young woman possesses great creativity and truly has a God given talent. The writing and storyline of this play had much to be desired. But Gloria gave such life to her character; I left with a longing to see this play over and over again'.*"

Gloria looked up and paused for a moment before speaking. "Wow! What paper is that from?" Looking straight at Gloria, Nell answered "I didn't pick it out; some guy at the stand just handed it to me as I was leaving."

"You're kidding?" Gloria said as she took in a deep breath and even though she had a grin on her face, still the tears fell down her cheeks. "What's the name of the paper?" She asked. "And what's the writer's name?"

"The paper is called *Abba's Bragging Rights Review,* and the writer just goes by the initials J.C."

The Angels Sang

Grace knew she was loved. From the day Tykera brought her home from the hospital she was the essence of life in their third floor one bedroom apartment. The sound of cars, busses, and roar of the transit train were a constant during the daylight hours, and at night add to that the occasional cursing from the neighbors behind the paper thin walls. But, this existence was heaven compared to life in the streets that included brutal beating by the hand of a pimp if the money brought in was less than expected. What was even more unexpected was the day Tykera was told she was pregnant.

The doctor's were able to stop the internal bleeding from the brutal blows that left her with bruised kidneys and a ruptured spleen. Against all odds the faint beat of a heart echoed from Tykera's womb. This gave her hope of escaping the life of illicit sex, drugs, and pain. It didn't matter that this conception was by a nameless man of moral disgrace. This was Tykera's "fork" in her life's road. It was now or never. The words of the nurse in the hospital that night kept coming back to her. Words that pointed out that her life was special and valuable. So valuable and so loved that God Himself sacrificed His son to make sure that she had hope for the future, she was loved unconditionally, and that she need not ever again face life alone.

The outbreak of desperate and extreme frenzy overtook Tykera as she trembled past each convulsion from withdrawal. "Just let me die!" was her agonizing cry as the hours of sweat and pain lead into days of restraint from her hospital bed. "Oh God, I can't do this!" She had no conscious awareness that prayers were coming from the nurse in the chair right beside her; prayers that were pleading for relief and life.

The unmistakable aroma of bacon came wafting into the room. Tykera breathed in with a sense of smell that for so long had eluded her. She focused her eyes on the surroundings in the room. Turning to the chair next to her bed she saw a box of Kleenex and an open Bible. "Well good morning Sunshine" the nurse said as she wheeled in the cart containing a plate of breakfast under a plastic dome. "If you eat at least some of this we can unhook your I.V. today." By hospital standards this was a basic entrée for breakfast, but for Tykere, this was a breakfast of champions.

"Well praise the Lord, look who lives" were the words that came from the smiling face of a stout but attractive middle aged woman as she entered Tykere's room. "Do I know you?" Tykera asked. "Yes and no" said the woman. She sat herself in the chair next to the bed and placed the Bible that was there in her lap. "My name is Althea." Then she gently gripped Tykera's hand and said "Now, do you know who you are?" Silenced filled the room as Tykera held back the tears of facing her own reality.

She bit her bottom lip for a brief second and faintly replied "I think I am going to be a mom. But I don't know how to do that. I don't have a job or no place to live." The facts were clear and on her chart that she had been beaten, endured detoxification, and was pregnant. But at this moment, knowing exactly who she was was not clear; at least not to her. With a sincere but deliberate voice, Althea responded "You my dear are here for a reason. God believes in you more than you believe in yourself right now. I can set you up on a road to support and provision, but you have a choice to make. You can either go forward on your own accord, but then again, how's that been working for you so far? Or, take a leap of faith by letting God's love let you live a life with purpose and power."

Hospital room 531 that day became the birthplace of Tykera, a child of God. After that prayer's 'Amen', Althea and Tykera embraced each other with tears of joy. At the same time there was an outbreak of song from rejoicing angels in heaven. Seven months later room 207 in that same hospital became the birthplace of Grace. Born that day was a child conceived from an act of violation, but named after the redeeming provision of freedom in Christ. Again, the angels sang.

Pumpkin Spice of Life

Some things are funny, and some things aren't. This is a story of something you might think to be funny, but really is not funny at all. It all started on a foggy fall morning in Orville. The hamsters in Kevin's room had already shredded their days' worth of toilet paper and were working on their breakfast of multicolored nuggets.

Orville is not a big town, but it has its share of big events that the town's people look forward to every year. One of these events is the annual Pumpkin Festival. For whatever reason, this morning the pumpkin shaped alarm clock next to Kevin's bed not only didn't ring for the daily morning wake up time; it apparently had made its last tick at around 11:46 pm. Not a good time for this timepiece to bite the dust.

Kevin needed that early morning start on his entry for the pumpkin pie contest. His pie had to be perfect, it had to be fresh, and it had to be on the judges table by 11:30 am. If it wasn't for Lulu and Ollie getting into a throw down scrapping fight over who knows what, Kevin wouldn't have woken up at all. "Ah, no!" Kevin screamed as his eyes focused in on the dead clock. All he could do was throw on his clothes from the day before and rush downstairs to get the oven heating up for pie time.

There was no time for a shower or even to brush his teeth. Just so as not to ruin his chances of offending the judges with *morning breath,* he grabbed the bag of peppermints from his mother's secret stash behind the sewing machine and stuffed them into his pocket. "Of all days for her to leave so early," Kevin thought to himself. But Mrs. Agnew came down with a gall bladder attack the night before and someone had to teach the Momma's Little Mermaids swim class down at the community center.

You might think that entering a pumpkin pie contest is a bit odd for a thirteen year old boy. But Kevin is not your ordinary boy. He knew what he wanted in life, and football or brutal video games did not make his list of what he considered fun. His infatuation for anything pumpkin seemed to have started one Halloween when he was just four years old. The streets were full of kids in costume filling their pillow cases or plastic pumpkins with candy. But when Kevin came home, he dumped out all of his candy into the bathroom sink and slept with his empty plastic pumpkin positioned on a pillow at the foot of his bed. Up until that day anything pumpkin that was to have crossed his lips, would have been immediately spewed out with a spit and a grunt. So when Kevin came down the next morning and announced that he wanted pumpkin pie for dessert that night; jaws dropped and the room went silent. "Okay, I'll make one today" said Kevin's mom as she watched her son react with delight with a grin from ear to ear.

Over the years Kevin took an interest in everything pumpkin and excelled in his projects from growing the largest one to perfecting a pumpkin pie recipe that was the envy of the town's reigning pie queen Ms. Metzgar. To this day his love for anything pumpkin is a mystery, but for some reason that hard orange vegetable brings joy to that young man, and because some think it's funny, it has also brought a thick skin to that same boy because he refuses to let others rob him of his passion.

If you're wondering what happened to the pie contest; that morning Kevin managed to whip together the world's best ever pumpkin pie and won by a landslide of accolades. The news of his winning pie spread across the land from one blog to another and finally reached the attention of the Libby's canned pumpkin company. They bought that pie recipe from him and with that, Kevin started a nest egg for his dream of opening a pie house at the edge of town. Nobody thinks he's funny now.

Flatline

"That squealing sound is vaguely familiar; but where is it coming from? Ah, there it is. Move over, Martin, I can't see it. Martin, Allie, Mom? Me? Wow, this is like in those medical shows where tubes, wires, and bleeping sounds all come to a dramatic stop with everyone staring at the flat line on the heart monitor screen. I don't remember this from last time though. I can see you all down there. Tyler? Are you here? I missed you too much, I didn't want to live anymore without you. I'm here, son, where are you?"

"Mom, I'm here."

"Tyler? Tyler, I can't see you. Where are you?"

"Mom, do you know what love is?"

"Oh. Tyler, I do. I love you. Where are you?"

"Have you always loved me? "

"Yes honey! So much you will never know. Where are you, sweetie?"

"I can see you Mom. You are beautiful. Your eyes shine as if light is illuminating directly from your soul. I know that light mom; I've seen Him."

"Tyler, are you alright? Where are you?"

"Mom, do you remember the car accident?"

"I can't forget the car accident. I lost you. I couldn't go on without you."

"Mom, going on is what life is about. I am meant to be here now, and here I am more alive than I have ever known. But it's not your time to understand this yet, Mom, you need to go back."

"No, I need to see you; I need to be with you. Tyler, where are you?"

***

The room was immediately filled with nurses madly calling out orders. As one injected something into the I.V. tube, another began CPR while waiting for the crash cart to arrive.

"Charlotte, don't do this!" Dad screamed as we were all escorted out by Irene; the night nurse. She brought us to the private room where only the families awaiting tragic news were sent. It's as if the fear and grief of death are too real to expose to those still hoping for the best. But this wasn't the first time we had gathered in this room and now any hope that we may have had was rapidly fading.

Mom had given up on life long ago regardless of all of our efforts to convince her otherwise. Remembering the past four years Allie thought to herself "Yes, I lost my brother, but I never really got back my mother again either. Why Mom? Why?"

Dad started to pray "Lord, we know she's yours, we know you hold the future, but give your healing power to Charlotte's body right now; please Lord." Grandma sat in the chair beside him and shook her head in her hands sobbing; breathing only with intermittent gasps for air.

***

"Mom, I'm right here." Tyler's image began to emerge from the stillness.

"Tyler, Tyler! I've missed you so much!"

"Look at me Mom. Do you see anything different?"

Charlotte could do nothing else but look at Tyler before she spoke words that she didn't understand. "You're my boy, but I'm sensing that my love is more my need for you than yours for me. My life without you was so vacant. But you're happy; perfectly happy. Why not me? I don't ever want to leave you again."

"You will, Mom, and that's okay, really. Look again, Mom, look at me."

"You're not mine anymore are you? I can see hands on your shoulders. I can see love from the light behind you. How does one see love, Tyler?"

"Love is, He just is. You can't hold me now just as He can't hold you now either. He loves you so much; He always has. For now you need to be there for Dad and Allie, and Grandma. That's just the way He's planned it. When you pray for the pain to go away, let it go away. Only then will your wounds heal and life can return. I never left you Mom; I just left life as you know it. Don't worry, a glorious reunion is coming, and it will be without any need for comfort or assurance. I was your son for a while, but you are His daughter. He waits for you while watching you grow too. You'll know His voice when He calls you."

***

"Charlotte? Can you hear me?"

"Martin, forgive me."

"Oh, Honey. We love you."

"Thanks for waiting for me. I love you all. I'm back."

<u>Front Pew Plays</u>

(Short Drama Scripts for the Church)

Nana's Christmas Gift

Synopsis: Before dying, Grandma *(Nana)* left for her children and grandchildren a letter explaining the last Christmas gifts that she would leave for them. The real gift is the legacy of Christmas past for Nana, but also a deeper meaning of Christmas and family to be treasured more than any store bought gift.

Setting: on stage right a Christmas tree and a living room chair on the left small table and chair for Nana to write on.

Cast: Nana, Daughter, Children (optional—may be assumed)

Props: *(2 of each item, one for Nana to put into gift box and one for the daughter to simultaneously pull out of her gift box)* Gift Box, Christmas Tree *(optional—may be assumed)*, table and chair, paper and pen, bag of microwave popcorn, car 'tree' deodorizer, bag of marshmallows, box of instant hot chocolate, bag of fresh whole cranberries, Glade candle *(gingerbread or cookie fragrance if possible),* package of seeds, Swiss Army knife.

The scene starts with the grown daughter assembling the grandchildren in front *(children may be present or assumed)* to read a letter Nana left them before she died.

Daughter: Okay, kids, be quiet and listen. We are going to have to get used to not having Nana here at Christmas time. But before she passed away she made sure that all of you had a special gift from her; and she wanted me to read this letter, i*f I can get through it,"(she mumbles under her breath)* "to all of you before you open your gifts." *(heavy sigh as she composes herself to read - she starts reading the letter and stops reading aloud as soon as Nana's part kicks in. But she continues to lip sync as if reading and utilizes the corresponding props as Nana reveals them in her lines. (this is an optional backdrop setting but can also freeze to only focus on Nana until the end when it goes back to the last lines read with the children setting)*

Daughter begins to read: "I write to you to share with you one last time at this Christmas. For soon the baby Jesus will no longer be just a story for me. When I get to heaven I will be sure to tell him to watch over all of you. But for now, I give to you each a gift of treasures."

{This is where the focus switches over to Nana (elderly and weak grandmother sitting at table writing this letter) the assorted goods are in one bag on the floor next to her. As she completes her description of each one she then puts that one item from the bag into a gift box}

Nana: *(speaking in an unidentifiable "old country" accent)* "Back when I was a little girl, we did not have the pop-up ready-lit Christmas trees that you have today. A week before Christmas Papa would go to the edge of town where there was a field of Evergreen trees. There were big ones and little ones. And every year Papa would find just the right one and cut it down to bring home for our living room. Oh how the whole house would smell of fresh pine tree. So for you I give one of these little trees that they hang in the cars; that maybe just a little you could enjoy the smell of trees that your Nana remembers or Christmas time." *(Nana examines and puts the air freshener into the gift box / at the same time the daughter pulls a tree air freshener from one of the gift boxes)*

"And we did not have the bright shining lights and glass balls that you have on your tree today. We would sit by the fire and with needle and thread sew together popcorn and fresh cranberries to string on the tree to decorate." *(Nana puts a package of popcorn and a bag of cranberries into the gift box - after placing in the box she resumes writing)* "If you make this for your tree someday be sure that there is no dog around to eat the popcorn off the string.

"While we did this, every year Momma would make for us some hot chocolate. This was the only time of the year that we got this. And once in awhile Momma would make marshmallows for in the chocolate. Yes, children, marshmallows can be home-made, but I don't recommend it. So I give to you some hot chocolate and a bag of marshmallows to make for when you as a family decorate your tree. *(The marshmallows and box of hot chocolate is placed in the gift box by Nana while the same items are taken out of gift box by the daughter in front of children)*

"I must tell you the story of the time when I was first married with children and I wanted to make the Christmas time so special. I had seen on the magazine a ginger bread decoration. This was not just a gingerbread house with the gum drops on the roof. No, this was a ginger bread covered bridge with a horse drawn carriage and some gingerbread children skating on a nearby pond. It was so beautiful and would make such a wonderful memory. Well, it did make a memory. I made that covered bridge, horse drawn carriage, and the children for skating on the pond. I had finished frosting them all with such beautiful colors and laid them out on the dining room table to dry while I went out to do some Christmas shopping. When I got home, the dog and the cat had worked together to knock the gingerbread figures off the table and they had eaten all of the children. Nowadays, you have from the Wal-Mart the ready- made kits to make the gingerbread houses, so again I don't recommend you make from scratch... so I give for you one of these Glades candles so that you can enjoy the smell of the gingerbread baking in the oven; which is really the best part. *(The Glade candle is used as prop here for the gift bags)*

"Anyway, every year Momma would retrieve from the fruit cellar a box of crab apples and would tie bows onto them to hang onto the Christmas tree for decoration. Then the night before Christmas, when we thought Momma and Papa were gone to bed, we the children would sneak down to the tree and take bites out of those crab apples. Later I learned that Momma and Papa were not to sleep, but would be watching from the kitchen door hoping that we would be biting the apples. For you I give a package of apple seeds so that you can grow the crab apples for your own Christmas trees. And I will be watching from heaven with a smile on my face to see who takes the bites out of the apples. *(A package of seeds are used as a prop for gift boxes)*

"You will be probably going shopping looking for just the right gift for each other. But back when I was a child, we did not have the malls or the Toys-R-Us. Weeks before Christmas we were told not to go out to Papa's wood shop until after Christmas morning. We all knew that he would be busy out there making from wood some special toy for us for Christmas. One year even though I did not dare go out to the wood shop, I knew that he was making for me a crib for the rag doll that Momma had made for me the year before. And of course that year I got the most wonderful crib that a little girl could ever dream of for her doll. Even though so many other beautiful things are now much easier for you to get for each other, I give to you a little carving knife to remember that what you give is not just a present that was bought, but comes from your heart as if you could have made it yourself." *(At this point Nana stops talking out loud)*

(The daughter pulls out of the gift box a little Swiss Army knife)

Daughter: *(still reading the letter)* "So my children, and my precious grandchildren, even though I will no longer be with you there, I want you all to know that you have been the gifts for me in my life that I will never forget. Love always, Nana

Try the Dip

Synopsis: Celebrations and sorrows are all a part of life. A part of life can also be a tendency for judgmental impressions. In this story both celebration and sorrow meet and judgmental assumptions are put in their place.

Setting: at a 25th wedding anniversary party

Props: table of party food (including chips & dip) tray of appetizers, small teddy ber, large purse and cell phone.

Cast: 4 actresses: Carol *(hostess),* Janet *(reserved personality),* Donna *(judgmental gossip),* Cindy *(Donna's friend)*

Carol: "Hi, Janet, I'm so glad you could make it. Come in, come in. Did you bring Stan with you?"

Janet: "No, he's staying home with the kids. But you were so kind to offer that I had to come over and to congratulate you and Rob on your 25th wedding anniversary. That is a big accomplishment now a days. And you have such a lovely home. Have you lived here long?"

Carol: "Oh my, yes. It's been 21 years out of our 25! We started off living in the basement of Rob's parents. And then when we moved here, well, it's just been home ever since. Come, I'll take you on the grand tour."

(Donna and Cindy enter, pour punch and loiter around the chips and dip)

Donna: "Carol always puts on a good spread. Yum, try the dip it's delicious."

Cindy: "Every year I look forward to the block party just to see what Carol has planned to bring us all together."

Donna: "Well, I tell you what, we willl never forget last year's block party. It was around that time we got the news that if Josh didn't get a new heart, he would never see another one of those block parties. A parent can never forget that feeling of panic and helplessness."

Cindy: "How's he doing now?"

Donna: "Since the transplant he has been doing so great. We have to keep him from overexerting himself."

Cindy: "Wow, that's terrific. Did you ever find out who the donor was?"

Donna: "No, but I heard the nurse down the hall say that the mother had mentioned that her daughter had a really big Teddy Bear collection. So, with that I know it was a little girl, and Josh has a Teddy Bear collection. too. So she must have had a tender heart as well."

Cindy: "Oh Donna, stop me, this dip is sooo good!"

Donna: "I know, we'll have to go another 30 minute round at Curves just to pay for this."

(Janet re-enters with Carol but Carol gets drawn back by the ringing of the kitchen timer / Janet seats herself and picks up a scrapbook to look at)

(Back at the dip)

Donna: "I'm going to see if I can help Carol out. Go check out the new neighbors. But good luck. She doesn't seem to socialize with anyone."

(Donna exits and Cindy approaches Janet)

Cindy: "Hi, I'm Cindy. I live down past Jensen's in the Yellow house with the toys and assorted tables of kid's clothes set up in the front yard as kind of a perpetual garage sale."

Janet: "Oh yeah, I've seen that. Hi, I'm Janet. So, that must be your little entrepreneurs huh?"

Cindy: "Yes, that's my boy and his sister. That little business of theirs is the only thing they seem to be able to collaborate on without someone ending up in time out. How about you? Do you have any children?"

Janet: "Yeah, uh.. two boys. They keep me busy. With the move and all it's been hard for them to settle in this late in the school year."

Cindy: "Yeah, yeah, it's hard. But they'll adjust in no time. Where did you move from?"

Janet: "Eurphrada. It's east of the mountains. It is a small community where everyone knows each other. Even though that may sound quaint, it has its drawbacks, too."

Cindy: "Was your husband able to find a job here? I know things are pretty tight here for work."

Janet: "He's taking a bit of a break right now. But he has been offered a transfer position available to him at the Haggen's south side store whenever he's ready."

Cindy: "Do you work?"

Janet: "No, I stay home with the kids."

Cindy: "Well, you should come over with the kids next weekend for my Sarah's 10 year birthday party. I think your boy is in her class. She is a Martha Stewart in the making... parties are her thing. The more kids there are the more she gets into it. What are your boys' names? I'll have Sarah make up some invitations for them."

Janet: "Oh, I don't think so, I…"

Cindy: "Oh come on, I promise not to let Sarah bamboozle you into being her hand model for her new sparkle nail kit."

Janet: "I better call home and see how Stan is doing with the boys." *(She pulls her cell phone out of her purse as she leaves)*

(Donna re-enters and matches back up with Cindy)

Donna: "Well, what's the scoop? Is she too good for the likes of us or what?"

Cindy: "I don't know, she seems nice enough, but she's kind of weird."

Donna: "Maybe she's in the witness protection program or something. Well, you tried."

Cindy: "Right off the bat, I don't think she would fit in at one of our girls' nights out. I think she's more the type that keeps to herself. Who knows, maybe if we got a Magnum bar or tow down her she'd talk."

Cindy & Donna: "NOT!"

Donna: '"Come on downstairs you've got to see this. Carol's kids have made a sculpture of her and Rob on their wedding day, made completely out of Spam."

(Cindy and Donna exit / Janet returns to put her cell phone back in her purse but is distracted by Carol who approaches her with a tray of appetizers

Carol: "Cindy, here you must try Rob's famous Hawaiian meat balls."

Janet: "Oh thanks so much, Carol, but I think I better get back home and relieve Stan from the boys."

Carol: "Janet, are you sure you don't want to just call him back and have him come over with the boys instead? There is plenty of food, and the kids have their own video games going on in the other room. You really should make breaks for yourself when you can."

Janet: "Thanks Carol, but I just can't keep up the pace right now."

Carol: "Well, whenever you're ready. This neighborhood really has some great people in it. I know what it's like to lose a child. My Mary was three when we lost her."

Janet: *"Again, thanks. Carol." (she sucks in a deep breath that holds back the tears and excuses herself without retrieving her purse)*

Carol: *(she calls out to Janet)* "You call me anytime you want. I mean it."

Janet: *(through tears)* "I will, I will…"

(As Carol closes the door Cindy and Donna return)

Donna: "Carol that is quite the likeness of you and Rob downstairs."

Carol: "Oh, those kids. I certainly didn't expect that!"

Cindy: "Did Janet have to leave?"

Carol: "Yes, she is just trying to breathe in and breathe out right now."

Donna: "What's going on? I assumed we're just not her kind of crowd."

Carol: "Oh no, she lost her daughter about ten months ago. That's why they moved away. But she is still in the grips of grief. You and she actually have a lot in common. You certainly can understand that pain. Let her know, maybe you are just the strength she needs to make it through this time. Especially since they had to make the decision before she died that they would participate in the donor program. Somewhere her daughter lives on. Donna, I'll give you her number. Call her."

Donna *(Donna nods her head in agreement)* "I will."

(As they walk past the chair where Janet's purse lay open, Donna notices it and picks it up. It opens to reveal a small Teddy Bear with a red ribbon around its neck. Donna pulls it out, looks at it and holds it to her chest and says under her breath):

Donna: "Yes, I will have to call her for sure. "

You Can Bank On Us

Synopsis: Based on the writing's of Paul to the Galatians that Christ died to provide all life and freedom and works were no longer had to be a part of the security of salvation. In this story two co-workers are met with a choice of where they want to put their trust in the not only now, but for later. One chooses that of security, but at a cost; and the other chooses security with peace of mind and freedom that he made the right choice.

Setting:

Center stage - an office water cooler

Stage left - a bank desk

Stage right - a bank desk

Cast:

Steve - guy who chooses saving account offer with Valley Free Bank

Josh - guy who chooses savings account offer with Okanagan Law First Bank

Banker #1 = Okanagan Law First Bank

Banker #2 = Valley Free Bank

Props: 2 office desks and water cooler.

(Starts off on center stage where both characters approach the water cooler)

Steve: "Hey Josh. How's your day going?"

Josh: "Pretty good, how about yourself?"

Steve: "Today I think I'm winning. Any plans for lunch?"

Josh: "Ya, I'm planning on going down to that Okanagan Law First Bank. I saw their ad on TV and it sounds like it is the kind of bank I can work with. So lunch time today I am heading down there to open a savings account. If you don't have a good savings account somewhere, you should come with me and get one there too."

Steve: "Ya, I saw that ad. But did you see the one for the Valley Free Bank? There are no fees for anything. It just seems like they are sincerely interested in my well-being instead of any kind of fee-based profit."

Josh: "Oh, I saw that ad and the first thing I thought was "there's gotta be a hitch." There is no such thing as free. Sooner or later when you least expect it, they will hit you with hidden fees, and then the games begin. No, I'd rather go in knowing what is expected of me and then there are no surprises. Sure, there is a fee for signing up, one for deposits, withdrawals, monthly and annual service fee, and of course a penalty fee for early withdrawals or overdrawn accounts. But you can't expect something for nothing now a days."

Steve: "I know, but there is just something about Valley Free that I feel I can trust my life savings with them."

Josh: "Well, that's free enterprise for you; everybody can make their own choices as to where they want to do business. I'm going to take my chances with Okanagan Law First. Plus, when I sign up I get a free toaster."

Steve: "Good luck with that. How about tomorrow we go for lunch at Montana's? They have a lunch special there that includes a salad bar and all you can eat ribs."

Josh: "Great! Sounds like a plan, tomorrow it will be." (*Gives a thumbs up and they both exit to separate bankers desks*)

Banker #1: "Good afternoon, sir, may I help you with something?"

Josh: "Yes, I saw your ad and would like to sign up for your savings account."

Banker #1: "Wonderful. I will just make you aware of all of our fees and expectations, and then all you need to do is sign up and make your first deposit. *(the banker hands him a thick stack of papers to go over)* Just initial here, here, here, here, here, here, here, here, and here. Fill this in with your complete name, address, phone number, mother's maiden name, your place of birth, social security number, driver's license number, car registration number, your clothing and shoe size, and any history of cheating in school, lying to your parents, and/or any preferred swear words that have been or may be expressed by you in the future."

Josh: "Wow, you don't leave any room for error do you?"

Banker #1: "No sir, here at Valley Law First we realize that nobody is perfect and in order for us to work with you, you have to work with us."

Josh: "Understood. If you are willing to work with me, I'm willing to work with you." *(With a nod of the head he signs the contract)*

Banker #1: "I'm sure for the most part, it will be wonderful working with you, sir. *(the banker stands and reaches to shake hands)* Oh, I almost forgot. Here is your free toaster." *(The banker reaches under the desk and gives a toaster to Josh)*

(Josh with a content gratified manor takes his free toaster, thanks the banker and turns to leave)

Banker #1: "Oh wait! Just one little thing about that toaster. There is no lifetime guarantee with that and from what I understand, no matter where you set the dials, it

WILL burn the toast every once and a while. You have a nice day now."

***

Banker #2: "Hello sir, welcome to Valley Free Bank. How may we help you?"

Steve: "I saw your ad and would like to open a savings account with you."

Banker #2: "May I call you by your first name?"

Steve: "Sure, it's Steve."

Banker #2: "Well, Steve, you will not regret your decision. We cherish our customer relations and promise to be here for you for all of your needs whenever you need us."

Steve: "Now let me just get this straight. There are no fees for ANYTHING?"

Banker #2: "No, Steve. Simply by you trusting your life savings with us, we consider YOU a part of the Valley Free family. We don't charge for our services because we as a family are there for each other. So far that has worked out very well. You can count on us."

Steve: "It seems so simple."

Banker #2: "It is, Steve."

Steve: "Can I take a look at the contract?"

Banker #2: "There is no contract at Valley Free." *(the banker reaches out to shake Steve's hand)* "A handshake is all we need from you to commit to us, and from then on our commitment is to you. What do you say, Steve?"

Steve: "I want to be a part of that." (He reaches over and shakes banker's hand)

Banker #2: "Welcome to the family of Valley Free."

Steve: "I know it sounds silly, but my friend is getting a toaster to sign up at another bank. Do I get any kind of free gift for signing up with Valley Free?"

Banker #2: "You can get a very inexpensive toaster down at any department store that you can use to make toast. But here at Valley Free we have your needs and your future in mind. We would much rather provide you with that security than a toaster that may last a year or two at best."

Steve: "That does make sense and it feels just right for me. Thank you."

Banker #2: "We know you will be happy, Steve, because here at Valley Free, satisfaction is guaranteed."

(The next morning Steve and Josh meet again at the office water cooler)

Steve: "Hey, Josh, so yesterday did you sign up with that bank?"

Josh: "Yeah, and got my free toaster too. How about you? Did you sign up for that "free" savings account at Valley Free Bank?"

Steve: "You know, Josh, I have a real peace about it. I think I made the right decision."

Josh: "To each his own."

Steve: "Are we still on for lunch today?"

Josh: "Ah, (sigh) no can do today. I have to go to the bank and make a deposit to cover this month's service fee or I will get charged for insufficient funds. Maybe tomorrow."

Hormone Relief Telethon

Synopsis: This skit was written as a promotion for an upcoming church women's retreat. Different aspects of what was to come at said retreat were weaved into the storylines of a fictional talk show with a very special guest. The theme song that is presented in this skit goes to the tune of the theme song written by Michael Jackson for the 1985 telethon benefiting the African famine at the time.

Setting: Talk show chairs and table with coffee cups for guests

Cast:

Ruthie: the talk show host

Mia Dahl *(meant to be pronounced My-a-doll; for the menstrual cramp medication 'Midol')* She is the arrogant, glitzy, Holly-wood type

Lady #1, Lady #2, Lady #3, and Lady #4

Choir of women - some holding head-phones to ears as they sing

2 people as audience plants.

Props: Cue cards with the theme song written on them (for the makeshift choir), can have some audience members be waving open lit cell phones, a handheld microphone for questions from the audience *(optional)*

Ruthie: "Today we have with us a very special guest. You may have seen her in such films as 'Hot Flash Dance', 'Water Retention World', or 'Not Tonighty'. She has also had hit albums with songs like 'In the Mood', 'Feelings, Nothing More than Feelings', and 'Girl's don't always wanna have fu-un'. Please welcome this very talented actress/singer, and now the creator and organizer of the upcoming 'Hormone Relief Telethn'…Mia Dahl."

(Mia enters stage and sits)

Ruthie: "Mia, thank you so much for being with us today. As if your schedule isn't busy enough with singing tours and movies, what motivated you to put together this telethon? Or as you refer to it 'HRT'."

Mia: "The suffering really. I have not only experienced it myself, but I see it every day in every walk of life. Women need to know that there is relief out there just for them."

Ruthie: "I understand that there will be some kind of satellite stations, so to speak, for this event. How is that going to work?"

Mia: "Yes, Ruthie. There will be individual (*hand gestures the quote signs for the word 'retreat'*) 'retreat' sites throughout the nation. It will be a time for women to get together and share the bonds of joy, encouragement, and nurturing that is estrogen."

Ruthie: "I saw that your sister was in the news recently. She also has a passion for suffering people. Will she be a part of this event as well?"

Mia: "Mary? No, Mary won't be participating in the telethon. As much as I love her, Mary doesn't quite grasp the big picture of things. Just as you saw in the news, she is involved with this Big Sister thing in her community. She is not going to be working with me because she feels she needs to be there for this one little girl. Who by the way is not even her real sister. I have been working with my dear friend, Martha who truly has an understanding of detail and has been my right hand through this whole endeavor. She herself endured the cruel effects of being confined in an environment of pure raw estrogen gone bad. But she survived and has joined with me to support this important cause. I am so excited that she chose to work with me when, in fact, she was also approached to do the Multiple Sclerosis telethon the same weekend. She said to me 'No Mia, just because I have the initials MS, doesn't mean I have to jump at every cause that goes by the same letters'. And we all love you for that, Martha." (blows a kiss to the camera)

Ruthie: "Now these individual retreat sites, Mia, will there be festivities of sorts happening at those as well as the show itself?"

Mia: "Oh yes, Ruthie. We have arranged for overnight accommodations in some of the most beautiful lodges - just perfect for reflection and inspiration."

Ruthie: "Well, let's open it up to our audience in case someone here may be interested in going to one of these retreats. Is that okay, Mia?"

Mia: "Oh sure, whatever you want to know… ask away."

Ruthie: "Ladies, are there any details that you want to ask about the telethon itself or one of these retreat locations that you could actually attend yourself?"

(*Planted people in audience to pose questions to*)

Lady #1: "Will meals be provided?"

Mia: "Yes, not just any meals either. We have flown into each of these sites the winning cooks of this year's Food Network Cook Off. Fabulous, trust me it will be absolutely scrumptious."

Lady # 2: "Will the menu include low carb?"

Mia: "Not really, but if you're concerned about that, portioning is always an option for you. The only 'low carb' item that will be there are rice cakes, but we won't actually be consuming them..We will have first class pedicurists there for anyone that would like to indulge in 'pretty feet', they will be using the rice cakes to sand off those nasty heel calluses. But of course for nutritional purposes all the food groups will be provided. And that includes chocolate."

Ruthie: "Oh? I didn't realize that chocolate was in one of the food groups."

Mia: "Yes, Ruthie. You see, chocolate is made from the cocoa bean and beans are a legume… so it really is a protein."

Ruthie: "Uh? I never thought of it that way."

Mia: "Oh yes, and the same goes for coffee as well."

Ruthie: "Well, when you factor that in, I eat a pretty healthy diet after all. That's good to know. Next question please."

Lady #3: "What sort of attire is suggested?"

Mia: "Whatever you are most comfortable in. To keep you up to date with the latest, there will be a fashion show as part of the program. There will also be hiking, hot-tubbing, and even a pajama party. And of course, everyone there will be wearing a "smile"… because we're worth it."

Lady #4: "Will there be separate entertainment provided for each location?"

Mia: "Yes. There will be everything from first rate theatre performances to demonstrations on decorating and scrap booking. And I have retained the top women speakers of the nation to share with us their insights and experiences of the essence of being a woman in today's world. Things like, the individual differences that we all possess, how we can embrace those differences, and maybe even expand the horizons of our lives. Differences like with such women as, let's say, Martha Stuart. The vitality and insights to detail that she can teach us. Compared to say, my sister Mary. Who uh, limits herself when she really has so much more potential to make an impact in our world."

Ruthie: "I hate to cut you short here, Mia, but we are running out of time and I understand that you have also written a theme song for this telethon. Any chance that we can hear that before we have to go?"

Mia: "As a matter of fact Ruthie, I have with me here today some of the celebrities that will be singing in the recording of this song. Right after this we will be going to the studio to tape it. So if we could go ahead and have them assemble right over there. we will give you a sample of the HRT theme song."

Ruthie: "Oh how special. Let's give Mia another big hand for being here and for being "there" for all of us women."

(Applause, applause, as Mia heads over to lead the choir)

<u>HRT THEME SONG</u>

(To the tune of We Are The World)

Choir:

"We are the women
We have the hormones

We can make a better day
Or make you miserable.
Misplaced my keys
Can't find my car now
But give a little time
And I'll turn on the charm now.
*(The whole choir chimes in / complete
with swaying)*
We are the women
We have the hormones
We can make a better day
Or make you miserable."

(This is where the choir quiets and Ruthie butts in to end the show)

Ruthie: "Thank you so much to our special guest Mia Dahl, and of course all of you wonderful women out there. See you next week."

(The singing continues)

"My moods can swing
From high to low now
There are more words to this song
But I can't remember them."

Trading Places

Synopsis: This skit is a parity of the home renovation show called Trading Spaces that aired on TV from the year 2000 to 2008. In each episode, two sets of neighbors redecorated one room in each other's home. The point in this drama is that although the two women neighbors that switch homes to renovate a room have completely different taste and perspectives on life, they came to appreciate that the differences are not always a bad thing and one should not be so quick to judge.

Setting: Is done in the style of Readers Theater.

Cast: Mary and Martha

Props: Two stools on stage - one for each woman / the women read aloud their letters to the producers of the show.

Mary: "To the producers of Trading Spaces, I would like to thank you for my new kitchen makeover. I don't really want to sound like I am complaining, but 'What were you thinking?' Don't get me wrong; Martha is a very organized woman. In fact I think that her middle name could very well be "Efficient," but her life is like her cooking... she measures everything. She incorporates only the finest ingredients, and then carefully blends them all together. Well, that's all fine and good, but what you end up with is stiff peaks. If God had intended for us to spend that much time in the kitchen, He wouldn't have created Kool Whip and Costco. Our newly designed kitchen is more like one of those perfect garages that has the outline of every tool on the wall so they will always be put back in just the right place. My children are actually afraid to touch anything. The other day my husband mistakenly put a coffee mug in the glass cupboard when a very loud alarm went off almost scaring him half to death. It's awful having anybody over anymore. Now after they leave, it takes me more time to put away the coffee cups in their proper place than it took in a whole evening of playing BUNKO with the girls. My house now has a different alarm for every cupboard. The other day I was going to make my children some soup. But because I was so afraid of setting something off by getting a pot out of the cupboard, I told them that movie stars eat soup cold. They call it Gazpacho. But I don't think they're going to buy the whole Steak Tartar thing. As you can imagine this fancy new kitchen is driving me crazy. I just don't get it."

Martha: "I would think that the producers of one of the nation's most popular TV home makeover show would have taken a more controlling position when dealing with a participant like Mary. You had to have seen that she is the type of person that lives moment to moment without a speck of preparation or planning. Don't get me wrong, I appreciate taking part in this wonderful adventure, but I had hoped that, regardless of Mary's perspective of what a kitchen should or should not be like, your people would have overridden her input for a more efficient and organized design.

"My new kitchen may look wonderful on the outside, but now the cereal cupboard is no longer divided into hot and cold cereals... they are all mixed up. Yesterday I found the Cheerios beside the Shredded Wheat. Maybe some people can live with this kind of chaos, but it is driving me crazy. I just don't get it."

Mary: "I understand that life with 3 boys has to be organized. But what's the fun in that? Martha is the kind of person that if she is not making sure that everyone's day is going according to schedule; she is off hosting a party for her kitchen gadget and alarm business. It's no surprise that she has all of her cupboards labelled alphabetically. There is even one labelled 'P' for articles made of plastic. Although, the change has made me think that I could possibly use a little bit more organization in my life. Maybe cereal could be a breakfast food instead of dinner. And I suppose that sometimes one could prepare a meal from scratch even if it takes over an hour. I can appreciate that all of what you have done is for my benefit, but I only have one question—does this new oven that you got us have a self-dusting feature like my old one?"

Martha: "I noticed that you combined the coffee cupboard items with the tea cupboard items. I also noticed that the two varieties of tea bags are now in one canister. I understand that the one tea canister does make a lovely display decoration, but now I have no idea when I reach for a bag of tea whether or not I will be pulling out a Jasmine tea or Orange Peko.

"At first I didn't think that I could live with this kind of uncertainty. But, I suppose I could use a little more spontaneity in my life. Why just yesterday I actually decided to try some of the frozen foods you so kindly stocked in my freezer. Believe it or not, I made a roast beef with Yorkshire pudding for dinner along with a Key Lime pie for dessert, all in just fifteen minutes. That extra time I had left not only allowed me to be at my son's after school hockey practice; I even spent some time filling in as goalie for them. This of course shocked my boys, but I must admit, a good time was had by all."

Mary: "Thanks to the organization in my kitchen now, I was able to find that super duper slicer dicer thing-a-ma-jig that I had gotten at one of Martha's kitchen gadget parties a couple of years ago. The last time I had seen it was when one of my kids was using it for a science project that had something to do with a salamander and seeing if its tail would grow back after slicing it off. And, I made a wonderful appetizer for our care group last week using a recipe I found in my new categorized and alphabetized recipe file. My family has noticed a remarkable improvement in the taste of my food now that the spice jars have all been properly labelled. I think I'm starting to get it, and..."

Martha: "With all of these new found conveniences, I have found that I am spending more time with my family. And to my surprise, I actually prefer that over preparing a perfect six-course meal. My husband was shocked but impressed that the other night, I had not only agreed to go out after dinner for Dairy Queen ice cream; I actually left the house without putting the toaster away… and it was still plugged in, too.

"I have recently become eligible for a Family Disney Vacation bonus package for exceeding my sales quota with a large and unexpected order of super duper slice dicers from the junior high school science teacher. Not only is the family excited about the trip, but now with my new found freedom of living life on the edge, I am going to let everyone pack their own suitcases. I think I'm starting to get it and…"

Mary & Martha: *(in unison)*: "Maybe this make over hasn't been all that bad after all."

Joy or Know Joy?

Background: This skit is a parity of a TV game show called '*Deal or No Deal*', which aired from 2005 to 2008 and was hosted by Howie Mandel. The object of that game was for the contestant to choose one briefcase out of a total of twenty six in hopes that the amount inside would be the top prize of one million dollars. But before that would be revealed, the contestant had to select by process of elimination to narrow down the briefcases left with the possibility that their chosen briefcase did indeed have the million dollars in it. As the dollar amounts are revealed by opening up chosen briefcases one at a time, their chances of winning the million dollars could be worth the risk; or if the million dollars was revealed along with the increments of dollar amounts, it is up to the contestant to regulate the game to go on or choose to see what their briefcase amount would be and thus take home that amount whether it be one dollar or ?? After each choice, the revealed card goes either on the side of Joy or the other side table for Know Joy *(May pin these up on a board so audience can see)*. At certain points of balancing possibilities, the host would pose to the contestant the question Deal or No Deal? Which left them to choose to either stop and reveal the amount in their briefcase, or take an offer of calculating cash to entice a deal or no deal that would end the game at that point.

Synopsis: This skit takes the game show to a similar but different level. By having the contents of the briefcases be an event that could take place in life, one would either have joy because of it, or because of it really know in their hearts the joy that comes from God's providence in our lives. Thus the 'Joy or Know Joy?' title.

This skit by itself gives the audience a look at things in life that have true, lasting meaning and joy that can only come by the grace of God.

But what happened when this skit was performed at the women's retreat, which it was written for, has been more of a blessing than by the way in which God in His plan anointed each element and timing of it. Be sure to read the story of what happened at the end of this script.

Setting & props: I had only twelve 'briefcases' – it happened that at the craft store there was an art kit that came in what looked to be a small metal briefcase. But lunch boxes could also be used. Behind each briefcase *(you will need 11 people for this)* a volunteer stands and opens the case when told to. Have three tables. The center table for briefcases and one table on one side for the collection of chosen 'Joy' cards, and one on the other side for the 'Know Joy' cards. Also have a tablecloth or curtain for two people to hold up that hides the final reveal.

You will need a cell phone for the host to call invisible mystery 'Banker'.

Heading signs for 'Joy' and 'Know Joy'

Cast: MC, 1 contestant and 11 models.

Host: "Welcome to the hottest new show today: Joy or Know Joy. A game where our contestant can be the recipient of

Joy beyond his/her understanding or dreams. Today we have with us (*name of person*) from (*city and state*). Are you ready?"

Contestant: "Yes."

Host: "Let's play. In one of those brief-cases is Joy beyond your wildest dreams. The others offer either Joy or to Know Joy rewards. Choose your briefcase."

Contestant: "Briefcase number 7!"

(Encourage audience participation to cheer on and clap - but prior to starting. select a plant in the crowd to yell out the given numbered cases that you have supplied for them. The contestant has been instructed to choose only the number that the audience plant shouts out)

Host: "Okay, *(name of contestant),* you know how the game works. You now choose three additional briefcases to see what your odds are of getting Joy. What are your cases?"

(Audience cheers on and plant shouts out the case to be chosen)

Contestant: "I choose briefcases numbers 5, 1, and 10!"

Host: "Now, let's see what is in those briefcases. Number 5." (*Gestures to the volunteer behind number 5 briefcase*) "Open your briefcase." (*She opens the briefcase and reveals case #5 which is a "Joy" event*): "<u>The IRS discovers an overpayment for the last 10 years and you receive $10,000 dollars.</u>"

(*The audience cheers and again the plant shouts out the next case to be chosen - which is case number 1*)

Host: "Open briefcase number 1.*"* (*Volunteer opens briefcase number one that says*): "<u>You have survived cancer and are declared cancer free.</u>"

(*The audience applauds and plant shouts out next number which is #10*)

Host: "Open briefcase number 10." (The volunteer opens the briefcase that says): "<u>A Royal Caribbean Cruise Line has chosen you as the winner of a sweepstakes for a 3 week Caribbean cruise.</u>"

(The audience applauds - a cell phone rings / the host pulls it out of pocket and answers it.)

Host: "Well, he told me to tell you this—if you are willing to give up what you have, he has a better offer for you. You will have to trust him."

(The contestant ponders / the audience encourages to go on)

Contestant: "Hmmm? Ultimate Joy has got to still be out there. No, I pass. Let's keep going."

Host: "Okay, choose 3 more briefcases."

(The audience encourages with applause and plant shouts out the cases)

Contestant: "I choose briefcases 2, 8, and 11."

Host: "Well, let's see if the ultimate Joy is out there or in #7." *(which is her chosen reserved briefcase)* "Number 2, open your briefcase." *(She opens to reveal)*: "Your nephew went missing while camping three days ago and he was just found safe and healthy."

(Audience applauds)

Host: "#8 open your briefcase." *(It reveals)*: "A brand new Mercedes SUV with a one years worth of gas."

"#11, open your briefcase." *(It reveals):* After six weeks of intensive care from delicate brain surgery, you take home a healthy baby girl.

(Audience applauds - the host's cell phone rings)

Host: "Mmm? That's interesting. He says to you that if you give up all of it he has an even better offer and for that you will just have to trust him."

(Audience encourages with applause)

Contestant: "No, I'm too close now. I got to find this for myself. I pass."

Host: "Let's play. Give me three more briefcases."

(Audience applauds and plant shouts out next case numbers)

Contestant: "#3, 9, and 4."

Host: "Is the Ultimate Joy out there or do you think that you have already found it? Number 3, open your briefcase." *(It reveals)*: "<u>You have been promoted at work and your salary is doubled.</u>"

"Number 4, open briefyour case." *(Which reveals)*: "<u>After years of being estranged from your mother, you resolve your differences and reconcile.</u>"

(Applause)

"Number 9, open your briefcase." *(It reveals)*: "<u>A promotional campaign for Merry Maids has selected you for a one year free house cleaning service.</u>"

(Applause - the host's cell phone rings. He/or she listens)

Host: "Okay, here is the deal… he says that if you give them all up except number 7, he will throw in #12."

Contestant: "Whhh-wow. Is it going to be worth it? (*Pause*) I've decided to trust him and accept his offer."

(Audience applauds)

Host: (*Addresses the constant this time and says*): "Open your briefcase."

The contestant opens #7 to reveal: "Un-conditional love."

(Applause!!!)

Host: "And now open # 12, please." *(It reveals*): "You will never be alone."

(Audience applauds - the contestant is overjoyed and hugs host)

Host: *"*Wow, those are quite the gifts you got there. Congratulations." (*Addressing audience*) – "And thank you all for joining us today on Joy or Know Joy."

(While these exit lines are being said, the briefcase girls lift the curtain to hide tables and put all of the briefcases now onto the Know Joy table... with #6 yet to be opened)

"And join us again for Joy or... *(the cell phone rings)*

Host: "Wait, wait! *(listens to cell phone)* Wow, this has never been done before! He says that because of your choice to trust him, you can keep what you have AND as an additional gift he wants you to have everything that is behind the curtain as well." (*The girls drop the curtain and all of the open briefcases are on the Know Joy table now plus the one un-opened briefcase*)

Host: "So, (*Contestant's name*) you have '*Unconditional Love*', and '*You Will Never Be Alone*'. Now it appears that everything that brought you '*Joy*', now you will also truly '*Know Joy*'. Plus there is that remaining case. I think since this gift is especially for you; you should be the one to open it... go ahead." *(gestures to contestant to step forward and open case that is on table.)*

Contestant: *(walks up to the case in anticipation stands in front of it to open it then steps aside to reveal)*: "Eternal Life."

Curtain - The End *(But in this case, not the end at all.)*

Post Script: Here is the story of how God anointed and blessed this skit:

Upon arriving at the women's retreat where this skit was to be performed, I randomly snagged a number of women to volunteer to be the assistants behind the numbered cases, and one gal to be the contestant. I did not know any of these women and just explained the simplicity of the skit was just to play along and that all of the details will be set up for them. The skit was going along splendidly. But when the contestant got to the reveal of the card that said: "<u>After years of being estranged from your mother, you resolve your differences and reconcile.</u>" She began to tear up. At first I thought "Good job, you must have acted before." Then towards the end of the skit where the card was revealed: "<u>Unconditional Love.</u>" And "<u>You will never be alone.</u>" She really started to cry. I thought that it made for a great showing of a contestant overjoyed with delight of winning. But, after the skit when I met up with the contestant gal, she told me that she actually was estranged from her mother for years and just a week before, had gotten together with her and mended their differences. Plus, her mother had been diagnosed with cancer and knowing of her limited life expectancy, she, by the guidance of her daughter, accepted Christ as her Saviour. So you can put it all together and see how God planned the whole thing for His glory. The bonus factor to this story that convinces me even more that God inspires writers is that the night before I decided to change the card that said "<u>After years of being estranged from your sister, you resolve your differences and reconcile </u>to <u>After years of being estranged from your mother, you resolve your differences and reconcile.</u>"

Selah

(a term often used in the Bible to suggest to the reader to stop and ponder what was just said)

Look for more hilarious works from Barb Miller in the future.